THE Power OF Motivation

INSIGHT PUBLISHING
SEVIERVILLE, TENNESSEE

© 2005 by Insight Publishing Company.

Published by Insight Publishing Company
P.O. Box 4189
Sevierville, Tennessee 37864

10 9 8 7 6 5 4 3 2

Printed in The United States

ISBN: 1-932863-65-6

Table Of Contents

A Message From The Publisher

I had a conversation recently with a sales professional who offered a hypercritical analysis of motivational speakers and the myriad of products they produce and sell in the marketplace. In short, he was a bit of a Scrooge. He wrapped up his diatribe by saying, "I don't need a bunch of professional cheerleaders to help me be successful!" I later learned that this sales professional was not having a banner year. In fact, he was struggling.

The facts are indisputable on this topic. Top performers in every field know how important it is to stay motivated. And, almost without exception, a part of their weekly routine centers on input from motivational experts—they listen to their tapes and CDs, they read their books, and they attend their live events. And because they stay motivated, they are able to successfully navigate through the common storms of their career. They survive and thrive when others throw in the towel.

In this dynamic edition of *The Power of Motivation*, we are proud to feature a rare collection of insights and strategies from some of America's most successful motivational experts. You'll find encouragement on every page!

David E. Wright, President
International Speakers Network

Chapter 1

Empowering The Business Profession

Terry Strom

Motivation. Do you have it? Can you get it? Does it already reside in you? I believe you make your own motivation by the choices you make and the actions you take. In this chapter, I am going to look at a principle that can either increase your motivation to succeed, or it can take away from that motivation. I will show that so much of what you do and do not do, is tied to how you perceive the events in your life. I believe that perception is reality—you can change your perception, and therefore you can change your reality.

Current or past negative experiences, if perceived correctly, can either propel you on to future success or, if perceived incorrectly, can hold you back. It's all in how you perceive what happened to you. The question to ask yourself is, "Do you perceive your setbacks or negative experiences as 'where you are now,' or do you see them as a platform to propel yourself forward?" I want you to know, from first-hand experience, you can learn to use these negative experiences—past or present—to propel yourself forward to success if you develop the correct perception about your experiences.

Have you ever heard the phrase "Perception is Reality"? I have been married to the same wonderful lady for over twenty years, and one of the most important things I've learned over those twenty years is no matter what I think I said, or how I think I said it, if my wife thinks I said something different, or she thinks I said it in a different way—I did. In my marriage, it's not what *I* think I said, it is what my *wife* thinks she heard me say that matters. If I could run around with a tape recorder during my entire married life, maybe I could prove her incorrect once in a while. But the point is, how you perceive your life to be is "how it is."

Another example is optical illusion puzzles. At one time you might see a vase in the image and at another time you see two faces. As you look at the image it switches back and forth between a vase and faces. Nothing in the image has changed, but your perception of the image makes you see different things.

Sun Tzu, a Chinese general living about 500 B.C. wrote the following account of a strategy of war: A general sent his army to invade another territory. When he came close to the country he was invading he knew that the other general would send out spies to determine how to attack his army. He gave orders on the first night to show 100,000 fires burning on the vast plain where his army was encamped. On the second night he ordered 50,000 fires, and on the third night only 20,000. The defending general pursued them hotly saying to himself, "I knew these men were cowards. Their numbers have already fallen by more than half." Needless to say, the defending general was thoroughly defeated because his perception of the invading army's strength was incorrect.

Early in my sales career, I would leave a follow-up sales appointment with what I term, "delayed intelligence," meaning I forgot to say something that with hindsight I thought would have closed the sale. The problem was I would remember it as I was driving away from the appointment. Early on when I did this, it would infuriate me. I would get so upset at myself and actually put myself down. However, as I realized that this was not helping me increase my sales, I decided to stop getting mad at myself and instead, learn from my mistake. After that, as I was driving away and realized I had just forgotten an important point I should have made, I would yell to myself, "Terry, did you learn something from the mistake you just made?" I would answer, "Yes." Then I would ask myself, "Are you going to do something different in the future as a result of what you just learned?" I would again answer, "Yes." I would then say out loud to myself, "Good, then because you have learned something from your mistake, you have become better. Learn from it and move on."

2

You can learn and grow from your mistakes and from your misfortunes also. Through this experience I have learned to look for even the smallest lesson I can learn from a mistake or misfortune. If I can find one way I can learn and grow as a result of the mistake, then I can change my perception regarding the event. I can change it from being a negative experience to being a positive experience. Wouldn't you like to have less negative experiences in your life? Using this method you can—by changing your perceptions from a negative experience to a positive learning and growing experience.

When I was a child I was the little, out-of-shape "pudgy" kid. My physical maturity was late in coming, and as a result I was not blessed with the six-pack stomach and bulging biceps or the coordination and agility of a fine athlete. I could not run far or fast, and lifting weights was an embarrassing experience for me. I was the "pud." I will never forget my sixth grade year. The teacher had all the boys line up at the horizontal bar to complete at least one pull-up. Well, I remember the fear I had as I waited for my turn. I watched boy after boy complete at least one, if not several pull-ups. I had never done a pull-up in my life. I went up to the bar with great trepidation. I jumped up and grabbed hold of the bar and then . . . just hung there, unable to pull myself up at all. I can still remember the laughter of the boys and girls who were watching.

Because of experiences like this in my early years, I became the kid to pick on and beat up. I remember a bully named Joe who used to box my ears in front of the whole class whenever the teacher went out of the room. He would challenge me to fight him; but I wasn't skilled in that area either. All of this led me to becoming the "nobody" in junior high and most of high school. It seemed that most kids in school were part of some group, but I was not. I was obviously not one of the jocks, or the socially elite. I was not one of the partiers, or part of the band, or drama club, or even one of the nerds. I was part of the "nobodies." I wasn't even called by my first name. No one referred to me as Terry, but as, "Oh, that's just S-T-R-O-M."

It's interesting that the lack of athletic ability in my youth and my lack of self-esteem pushed me and lead me to improve myself—this is what I want all of you reading this to take from my experience. Your defeat can become your gain if you will not be defeated by it. You can fall down a thousand times, but you're not defeated until you stop getting back up.

As a result of this lack of athletic ability and my low self-esteem, in the ninth grade I was walking home from school one day and I saw an overweight boy my age who was smoking a cigarette. I looked at the boy and he was wearing a white t-shirt that was pushed out in the front by a fat belly like mine. He had a pack of cigarettes rolled up in his right short sleeve like mine, and he was smoking a cigarette like I was. He looked terrible. I asked myself, "Do I look like that?" Of course I looked just like he did, right down to the pack of cigarettes rolled up in my sleeve. This realization affected me so intensely that I went home, threw away my cigarettes, and made the decision to get in shape. From that day forward to this day I never acquired the habit of smoking cigarettes and I've made a commitment to stay in shape.

This realization—this realistic view of myself—came at the end of the school year. As a result, that summer I started jogging and working out with weights regularly and joined a swimming club. At the end of the summer I joined the water polo team at my high school and continued to get in very good physical condition. I went from the boy who couldn't do one pull-up, to the boy who did twenty-two pull-ups at one time; from the boy who ran out of breath if he ran one one-quarter mile lap, to the boy who could run fifteen miles in the local mountains, or bike-ride 120 miles in one day. I went from barely being able to bench press fifty pounds to the young man who at 170 pounds could bench press 315 pounds of free weight. I went from the boy with twenty-five percent body fat down to one with ten percent body fat. I was never the national champion type of athlete, but I was able to change my situation by hard work. As a result I moved to the top five percent of physically conditioned people, and have continued to stay that way throughout my life.

There are so many people who feel stuck and cannot make any headway. The famous words, "men live lives of quiet desperation," have never been more true than they are today. The constant bombardment we get from the media of the many people who are "making it rich"—from movie stars to professional athletes—makes us "regular humans" look like total failures in comparison. But instead of trying to compete with the one thousandth of a percent of the people who make it super big, set your goals to something within reach. Envision a success story you have a real chance of winning. Then later, as you make headway to greater success, reset your goals to a higher level.

What is the motivation that propels people to excel even in the toughest of circumstances? How do they change their perspective to one of good when something so catastrophic has happened to them? I call these people heroes because they're willing to brave the worst life has to throw at them and still make a positive situation out of devastating circumstances. The world is full of heroic stories. Some are universal that everyone knows, and some are deeply personal. Most of the time only those who have achieved their own level of success know their story. Sometimes the best thing that can happen to you is adversity. It makes you perceive life differently and gives you an opportunity to take up the challenge to change things and make life better for you and those you love. Are you a hero? Could you become one?

There is a famous painter named Chuck Close who has been quite successful and has made a lot of money, the result of a stellar career in the art world. On December 7, 1988, at the age of 49 he suffered a debilitating spinal blood clot that left him paralyzed. The clot was in the upper part of his spine; an inch higher and he would have been dead; an inch lower and he might have recovered. During months of therapy his wife encouraged him to paint. But he was only able to paint with a brush in his mouth. He had someone Velcro small frames of canvas on his lap and he made tiny abstract paintings. He lined them all up on the wall in a grid. He realized that he could still produce the large paintings he used to do if he just painted small areas of a larger painting one square at a time. He took Polaroid pictures of people and scratched a grid onto the Polaroid. He had a slot made in his studio floor so that he could put a very large canvas down in the slot and get his wheelchair next to it. He painted a grid on the large canvas and for each small square on the Polaroid picture he painted a corresponding little abstract painting in the square on the canvas. With his wheelchair inches from the canvas he couldn't see the overall painting; he could only see the little square he was painting at the time. But when the canvas was raised from its slots in the floor and he rolled back to the other end of the studio, the full portrait emerged from the individual tiny paintings.

Everyone has to face hard times occasionally, and some times are obviously harder to face than others. Some of us overcome these hard times and some of us fall into despair because things look as if they will never get better. Chuck Close decided to change his perception of what had happened to him into a challenge he could win. His strength should encourage us; Chuck is a hero because he never considered giving up. He had to work very hard under difficult circumstances to create a life that is an inspiration to many others.

Luckily most of us have much less of a challenge to meet when we consider the path to our own personal success. One of the great challenges I had to face going through college to obtain a bachelor of science degree in engineering was that the job market for my branch of engineering was hiring very few people—only students with the highest grade point averages were getting jobs in their major. The rest were ending up getting jobs outside of engineering.

My problem was that I was just a B and C student throughout my high school years, and I couldn't see a way for me to graduate in the top part of my class. I realized that what I did not have in brains and connections I could make up for in determination; but I had to learn how to work hard. Hard work was not one of my talents at the time. Before every test, I decided to do every homework problem three times. This was not rocket science, but it got me A's on my test scores. It also meant I had to do every homework problem so I would know how to do them all correctly. I ended up spending at least twice as much time studying as any of my classmates. When everyone was partying on Friday nights, I was studying. Additionally, I worked the graveyard shift at a grocery store on Friday and Saturday nights so that I could spend all day and evenings studying Monday through Friday. It was not easy or fun, but I got straight A's in my major, and graduated second in my class. I got one of the highest paying jobs in my engineering discipline when I graduated, so my strategy worked. I have a saying about goals, and what it takes to achieve them, "If you work hard—it works." As you can see, I changed my perception regarding my situation and turned it into a challenge to be overcome.

A lot of my motivation for working hard and achieving (or some might say over-achieving) was a result of wanting to overcome the negativity of my early life. I wanted to prove to myself and to everyone else I could succeed. I've continued to tell my four children that I want them to enjoy their childhood; my wife and I have done our best to make that happen. It's sad that so many people do not enjoy their young lives. I will never forget the feeling I had when I walked on to the California Polytechnic University, Pomona campus for the first time. You know what I said to myself? I said, "This is the best day of my life, because I can start again—no one knows Terry Strom here." Wow! Would you want your child to say that? That was a turning point—I changed my perception about my life and decided to start over.

Part of the negativity in my young life was due to my low self-esteem and negative interaction with my peers. A lot of it was because of the lack of a strong supportive relationship with my primary male role model—my father—as a child and teenager. My relationship with my father is wonderful now; but both he and I wish it had been much stronger during my formative years.

Some people, like my wife, are fortunate enough to have had a nurturing and loving childhood, and perhaps they have less to overcome on the road to their success. But many people like me have had exactly the opposite type of childhood. It is unfortunate that I meet so many people from broken homes who grew up in hostile, unloving, and unsupportive families. Even though the challenges I had growing up were very important to my success later in my life, I don't wish my childhood on anyone as a way to become successful because it was so painful. I know there are many young people who have committed suicide during their teenage years because of their painful childhood.

For some, this adversity creates strength the way the high winds on the side of mountain create an extremely strong, but gnarled tree. I am that extremely strong, but gnarled tree. I say this to give hope to those who have gone through or who are currently going through the fire of adversities in life. I want to let you know that if you can learn and grow from these adverse experiences, you can become stronger than those who never had to go through them.

Even though my story is unfortunately quite mild in comparison to the lives of many young men and women in this day and age, it's the life template for so many people who end up living out their lives with low self-esteem and very little belief in themselves. Some people like me have been able to use this negative part of their lives to empower them to do better; but too many never get past a hard childhood. These are some of the people I'm writing this for. I want them to know they can use their past negatives as fuel to move forward. They can make a decision to leave the past behind and never look back.

In the following story, I got what I expected. It was a direct result of my perception at the time. What I expected was to get the job. When I was fifteen and a half my parents split up. At that time I was on the high school water polo and swim team. I knew we had very little money and owned a 1963 Impala station wagon that was not doing well. We also had four boys in the family; I was the oldest. I worried about the finances; I knew we needed money for another car, so I decided to drop out of the water polo and swim teams and get a job.

When I mentioned this to my peer group, they all said that this was a very bad time to get a job because there were no jobs to be had.

I really needed a job, so I changed my perception from the glass being half empty to being half full. I surmised that the reason my friends had not found a job was because they had not looked hard enough. I made myself do the uncomfortable thing—talk to every small business owner in the area who hired teenagers until I found a job. During the next two weeks I faced my fears many times by knocking on doors at small businesses all over town. As a result, I didn't get one job, instead, I was offered *three* jobs!

In my sales training seminars I teach that to get your sales businesses started you must live in the "land of uncomfortable" for a year. This means you must do things you don't want to do now, so you can have the life you want to live later. My wife and I have a saying, "We will do today what others will not do, so we can live tomorrow the life that others will never live." Can you see a parallel with my story about getting a job?

In life many people tend to rely on the opinion of others. But I've found that most other people do not want you to do well. Think about it. If your neighbor just won $100 million dollars in the state lottery, would you really be happy for him or her, or would you have wished that the lucky winner of that lottery lived 100 feet to the other side of your neighbor's house—at *your* house?

In life, it seems everything is relative. You have a nice car until your friend gets a better car. You have a nice home until your friend gets a better home. Perhaps the most relative factor is your salary. You may think you have a good salary until your friend gets a better job with more pay than you have.

There is an invisible scale we all have; it's a scale based on relative benefits versus wealth. Let's say you've been working in a job for ten years and as a result you have moved into a neighborhood populated with other people who make about the same salary you make. You decide to move on and start your own business with a much higher potential for income and freedom than your present job has and, as it turns out, better in the same way than your neighbor's job as well. You then tell your neighbor how excited you are about your new business, and what does he say? Well, he can do one of three things: 1) he can congratulate you and encourage you (unfortunately, few people will respond this way); 2) he can take it as a challenge and find a way to compete with you, so he doesn't get left behind, or 3) he can consciously or unconsciously try to discourage you (regrettably this will in many cases be the most common response). In the third scenario, your neighbor may not be willing to work hard enough on his own to try and progress along with you, and he may not want to congratulate or encourage you because he's afraid that if you succeed you will move ahead of him financially. In his mind he may (relatively speaking) move behind you financially which does not make him feel good (even though his situation has not changed). In this scenario, instead of encouraging you he dashes your dreams and tells you something like, "that will never work," or, "too many people are already doing that," or, "I know people who have gone broke doing that."

When you're starting something new, you don't need negative input, you need positive affirmation. Understand, this is not necessarily bad, it's just reality. Be careful when you ask an opinion of a friend or acquaintance—you may get the same response I did when I asked my high school friends about finding a job.

Again, perception is reality. If you think you can be successful at a new job or business, then you need to stack the cards in your favor. You are the most important person who must believe you can be successful; not your negative friends or acquaintances. If their negative comments can change your perception so you no longer believe you can be successful, then your perception—now your reality—will be that you cannot be successful. Be careful whom you listen to.

One of the major stumbling blocks to success is the perception that what is needed to be done to move on in life can't be done. This lack of self-confidence can be a tough wall to break through. At some point you have to start. Sometimes change is frightening. On the other hand, staying in the same place where you're unhappy is not a viable alternative either. Keep in mind the saying my wife and I have, "I will do today what other people will not do so I can live tomorrow the life that others will never live."

The most important thing is, *you have to begin*. Nothing will happen unless you start. I like the saying, "You miss 100 percent of the shots you don't take," so start taking them.

Having four children in team sports at one time brings with it numerous requests by the different leagues to coach a team. Therefore, I did a lot of coaching for soccer, baseball, and basketball, and I remember, specifically for soccer, that the more shots on goal the kids took, the more goals they eventually made. The same is true with each of you when you're trying something new—if you want to be successful, *you need to start*. Do something, and take a shot at the goal; otherwise there is no chance of scoring.

Do what you can do, but do it *today*. Don't be afraid to reach, it will get easier. Remember that you can only do something for the first time once. For example, many people—including myself when I started out—are very fearful of public speaking. However, because of my need to make speeches to increase one of my businesses, I had to force myself to go out and speak in front of groups, even though at the time it scared the "heck" out of me. The first time I spoke to an audience of nine people, "boy" was I scared. But you know what, I was never that scared to speak in front of nine people again. Then I had to speak to an audience of fifty people, and again I was scared big time. After I spoke in front of that first group of fifty people, it was never as hard to speak in front of that many again. I continued to speak in front of larger and larger crowds going through the same routine of apprehension and then confidence until I reached my first speaking engagement involving an audience of 15,000 people at a large arena. Man, I was scared more than ever! But, just like clockwork, once I spoke in front of those 15,000 people once, it was never as hard to do it again.

This rule can apply to almost anything new and scary you are encountering in your life such as your first interview, your first sales call, your first proposal, or your first business start-up. Once you begin performing tasks that scare you, you'll move closer to your goals. Those tasks will become easier and your confidence in yourself will grow; your perception about them will change. Always remember, action creates optimism; inactivity creates doubt and pessimism. To reach your goals, first start doing what's uncomfortable, then keep doing it and it will become more comfortable over time.

Another perception you must change if you're going to be successful in business and in life is the perception that "things never work out for me." Many people have this perception and it robs them of the personal power to get started on a project, or to continue working hard and stay doggedly persistent on a project until success is reached.
Because of this, if a person is not successful right away, he or she will not have the persistence to keep going. As a result, as I will illustrate in a moment, "the clutch will be dropped too soon." If you force yourself to change your perception from negativity to, "things work out positively for me and I am going to win," you have a much better chance of staying the course and being successful.

When I was 16 years old, the first car I bought was a 1971 Ford Pinto with a 1600cc four-cylinder engine. If your first car was at all like mine, it stalled a lot. I was broke and could not afford to fix it or purchase another car, so I nursed it along by continuing to push-start it. There's an art to push-starting a car—you have to start by pushing the car from a dead stop. This is the hardest part because you have to strain to get the car in motion. Then you need to have a friend in the driver's seat steering the car and holding the clutch in until exactly the right moment when the car has enough speed. Then, when you yell, "drop the clutch," the engine starts and the car continues on under its own power.

The problem is that if the clutch is dropped too soon by either not pushing the car hard enough to get sufficient speed (consider this hard work for our example), or you yell "drop the clutch" too soon, then the car will lurch to a dead stop. You then have to start pushing the car again from a dead stop (which is the hardest part), and go through the whole procedure once more. If your goal is to get to the end of the block, you could do it right the first time by pushing the car hard enough and fast enough (hard work), and continue pushing (being persistent) until the car can run on its own. Or, if you like to waste a lot of energy and get very frustrated, you could continue to drop the clutch too soon and continue to push-start your car many times within the same block. Because you continue to drop the clutch too soon your car continues to stop suddenly and you strain to push again and again. Now your destination seems very far away indeed.

People who do *not* change their perception that, "things work out positively for me and I am going to win," and who continue to believe a perception that, "things never work out for me," end up not working hard enough on their business endeavors for them to succeed. They quit too early because they perceive that no matter how hard they work, or how long they work at it, they will not succeed. People like these can only succeed if they experience very quick success; they get discouraged easily. But success seldom happens quickly. These people continue to fail at business ventures because they continue to start and stop, start and stop, and never build up enough momentum to become successful; just like my example of push-starting the car many times needlessly in one block because the clutch is continually dropped too early.

Here is an example of how this can happen in the sales arena; this can happen in almost any type of business endeavor also. If sales people want to increase their level of sales, they will have to fill the proverbial "hopper" or "funnel." The funnel is wide at the top and very narrow at the bottom. The bottom is where the closed sales come out; but to get closed sales to come out of the bottom of the funnel, you need to fill the much wider top with many potential buyers.

Let's say you're an insurance salesperson, or real estate agent, or in some other type of sales position. You get started with your leads. You are prospecting, sending out letters, cold- and warm-calling, contacting the decision-makers, qualifying the potential buyers, giving the sales presentation, and conducting the follow-ups. You are doing it all. You know it takes a few months to really get a solid flow of new business, so you're cranking it for the first week, the second week, and the third week—you're filling the hopper. But after a few weeks, you've not closed a sale or maybe you've closed just a few; and you become discouraged. You then do the absolute worst thing you could do—you back off before you have the amount of sales you desired. You stop adding new potential buyers to the top of your funnel, and the flow at the bottom of the funnel slows to a trickle.

What you've done is dropped the clutch too soon and your sales stop or never actually get started. As a result, your self-confidence and posture have decreased making you less effective. Now you have to start all over again with an even worse attitude and remember, the hardest part about push-starting your car is at the very beginning when you have to lean heavy into it by pushing to get the car moving from a dead stop. In the same way, the hardest part of the sales process is the very beginning when you're doing the prospecting, sending out letters, cold- and warm-calling, and because you dropped your clutch too soon, you have to do it all over again.

Let's say you dropped the clutch too soon and stalled your car when you were just a block away from your destination. If you had continued to push your car and waited to drop the clutch at the right time, you would have arrived at your destination much sooner with a lot less effort. In the same way, if you had continued filling your sales funnel it would not have been too long until the closed sales started pouring out the bottom. But because you stopped too early, those sales are now far away. If you had continued putting more potential buyers into the top of your hopper and had kept moving them through your sales funnel, the more sales you would have made, the more confidence you would have gained, and your sales process would have become better. If you do the process correctly, your potential buyers would start to realize by your confident posture that you do not need their sale because you have many potential buyers you're dealing with. In fact, you now start to change your perception from, "I hope someone buys," to, "I know someone is going to buy but I don't know who and I don't care who, I just know someone is going to buy."

This position gives you more power, because you change from being a needy salesperson to a confident salesperson who has more sales than you can handle. This type of attitude is extremely powerful in closing sales and can be used powerfully in many areas of business and life. The best thing to do is change your perception from, "things never work out for me," to, "things work out positively for me and I am going to win." Continue to persist and don't drop the clutch too early.

To prove my point that proper perception, persistence, and hard work are the main ingredients required for success in this world, let me share this story with you. When I was just about to graduate from college, I had been interviewing but I found I had missed meeting with the highest paying company interviewing students on campus that year, because I was off campus interviewing with another company. I went to the career center and asked about interviewing with the company and was told it was too late. I asked for the phone number of the interviewer anyway, which they gave me (remember—you miss 100 percent of the shots you don't take). I called the interviewer and he said they were no longer interviewing. I told him I would be in Los Angeles for another interview the next week, and asked him if it would be all right for me to stop by and meet him. He said "Sure, if you want to." I went to his office the next week and asked to see him. I waited quite a long time, but eventually he came out and said, "I'm sorry but I don't remember talking to you." I handed him a summary list of the straight A's in my engineering classes. He got excited and secured an interview for me that morning—I received an offer by that afternoon! This is a perfect example of hard work and persistence working together. If I had not worked hard on all my class work, had not earned straight A's in my core engineering classes, if I had not been persistent and not perceived I could get the job, I would have given up on getting the interview, and I would not have landed the job. As it turned out, this company only hired two people from my graduating class—I was one of the two.

The phrase, "Men lead lives of quiet desperation," is largely a result of dissatisfaction and fear. Both of these are sources of depression and loss of drive and energy for many. However, if financial fear and dissatisfaction have been defeating you, I encourage you to change your perception about them from being bad to being good. Change your awareness so that you see a potential benefit in the ability to drive you to change your situation. Successful people feed off financial fear and dissatisfaction, because they know that their body and mind will always try to move them away from pain, and financial fear and dissatisfaction do not feel good. Perceived properly, financial fear and dissatisfaction can actually be a very powerful influence that forces you to change your situation for the better.

When I was in junior high, I had a very good friend whose father owned a business on a street called Holt Boulevard. This was a very low-income area, and one of his father's employees was a very nice man who lived in that area. My friend and I spent many fun-filled afternoons with this employee and his family during the summer; but I remember having the feeling that I would never want to live there.

Well, just a few years later my father and mother divorced. This transition put a very heavy financial strain on my mother who was raising four boys. My dad—a truck driver—and my mom who was a stay-at-home mom with no work experience meant we were not financially well off *before* they split up, and now we were even worse off financially *after* they split up. Here I was a sixteen-year-old son of a truck driver with no skills, and no money to pay for college. The question came to my mind, "Would I end up on Holt Boulevard?" I realized something right then—I would never be content to live a life like my father and mother who had no education, an unhappy marriage, and were always low on money. Because of the fear I had for living in an area like Holt Boulevard, I decided that I would do whatever it took to always have enough financial resources to never have to live like that. This dissatisfaction and fear compelled me to excel and succeed in school, in my early engineering career, in my international direct sales company, my real estate development business, throughout my time in executive management, and even now in my speaking and corporate consulting business. Because I want a better life for my family and myself I keep striving because of the dissatisfaction I had with my parents' life and my fear of Holt Boulevard.

One of the most common of all perceptions is, "I am too old." In this day and age when we are inundated with media showing all these perfectly in-shape, beautiful actors, actresses, and models in their twenties, even being a person in their thirties can seem old. It gets worse for the people in their forties, fifties, and beyond.

We've all said something like, "If only I knew at twenty years old what I know now, then I would have done this or that." I used to hear myself say this as well, and then I thought, "Well Terry, you *do* know now what you know now, so why don't you apply that knowledge today?" Some of you believe you are too old to apply that knowledge, but do you realize how much longer people are living productive lives now? My grandmother is in her eighties. She speed-walks five miles and does yoga every day and has been doing this for as long as I can remember. My mother is in her sixties and rides her bike over 100 miles per week every week. She recently rode her bike over the pass in Glacier National Park, which is very steep and very high in elevation. And let's not forget to mention all the seventy- and eighty-year-olds who are competing in marathons and triathlons.

I was recently talking to a male friend of my grandmother's who is over eighty years old. He told me that most people he knows who did nothing productive with their lives after they retired died much younger than he is now. As a result he feared retirement more than working later in life. I'm finding that many retired people who can afford not to work are going back to work or starting their own businesses because they want to stay actively involved in life. Perhaps right now you are forty, and maybe you're considering that you can be ready to retire comfortably at fifty-five, sixty, or sixty-five. After you take all the trips you want to take in the first few years after retirement, do you really want to retire to a rocking chair? Or do you want to be involved in life in a productive way, even if it is just part time or volunteer work? I bet most of you would say "yes" to staying involved in life. My wife has a grandmother who lived to over 100 years old; so think about it, if you retire at sixty, travel heavily for three years then, based on her life, you would have thirty-seven years left to live. Wouldn't you want to do something interesting and productive with at least some of your time during those thirty-seven years? Add on top of that the fact that people who keep their minds and bodies active after retiring seem to live longer with more of their mental and physical facilities intact than those who do not.

Let's take it another step. You are forty years old and you're saying to yourself, "I wish I knew at twenty what I know now, because I would have done whatever (you fill in the blank)." Do you realize that you have potentially sixty more years to live? Many people have become multi-millionaires and even billionaires in their twenties and thirties. Keep in mind these youngsters did not really get started on the road to riches in most cases until they reached a minimum of eighteen to twenty years old. Take into account that they only had five to ten years of adult level experience and responsibilities to learn from before they became successful. Wouldn't it make sense to assume that you could take all you have learned in your forty years of life (twenty years of which were as an adult), and in the next ten to twenty years also create a financial empire for yourself? That would still leave you forty to fifty years of life (assuming you lived until you were 100) to enjoy the financial rewards you created "after" forty years of age. You can see that whether you are thirty or seventy, you still have a lot of time left to gain financial success and enjoy it.

To prove this point, think of all the people who have made huge successes in their later years, such as: Sam Walton of Wal-Mart, Ray Crock of McDonalds, and Winston Churchill, and, if you've seen any pictures of the Yosemite Valley, then you have seen the work of Ansel Adams, whose success also came later in life.

Ansel Adams was one of the most famous photographers who ever lived. When he was forty-two years old he photographed one of his most famous pictures of Yosemite Valley. Some of his most famous works, however, wouldn't come until he was in his sixties. And he continued to make images into his seventies. It took a lot of time, education, and practical working knowledge to get to a point where he could achieve success. Ansel Adams learned from what he did in his first forty years of life to make him great in his next thirty years. You can do the same.

I've heard it said, "You don't get what you think you ought to have, you don't get what you desire, you don't get what you struggle for, but you get what you expect." In reality, these are requirements to succeed in life. However if you're doing all four of the above listed items except expecting to win, in most cases you will not succeed.

How you perceive your abilities and your expectation of whether or not you will succeed in an endeavor will determine your effort and enthusiasm for what you are doing. And this ultimately will determine if you will succeed or fail. This means that your perception also ultimately determines your outcome, good or bad. This is so important, because what you believe about how well you will do at something will also determine how much effort you will put into it.

For example, you're going to start a business selling XYZ. If you do not believe you can sell XYZ, you will not spend much time trying to sell it because you think it will be a waste of time. As a result you will have very little enthusiasm which hurts your sales effectiveness and makes it harder to sell. When you encounter an objection, since you already do not believe people will buy it from you, you do not try to overcome the objection. Instead, you say to yourself that they will never buy XYZ from you anyway, so you just say, "Okay, thank you for your time." As a result of your perception that you cannot sell XYZs, you just lost a potential sale. If you end up not selling any XYZs right away, you may decide to quit because you think you can't do it anyway, so why waste any more time on it? However, if you change your perception to believing that you *can* sell XYZs, then you will be very enthusiastic and spend as much time as you can selling it. When you get an objection, because you believe that you can sell XYZs to anyone, you not only answer the objection, but you also fish for other objections that the potential buyer has. You answer all the objections up front and close the sale—you make the sale because you expected to. You would have been completely surprised if they had *not* bought from you. It's easy to see how your perception can change your result.

Do you ever compare yourself with others, and come up short? Do you ever wish your circumstances were different? Do you wish that life had turned out differently, or you had made different decisions? Do you ever think no one else is going through the challenges you're going through or that someone else got more breaks than you? Do you ever feel that if only this challenge or that situation would just resolve itself, then you could finally move on? Well if you do, join the majority of the human race. There is a difference between those who are successful and those who are not. The ones who are most successful have a perception that life happens for good or for bad; but they also believe they can and will move on in spite of life's challenges. They understand that the most successful people in the world have had major challenges and become successful in spite of those challenges.

You must understand that you are where you are right now; it could be good or it could be bad. If you want to better yourself, you will need to start from where you are and move on. You must accept this fact, or you really have no other option than to accept defeat and stay in the same place. Is that what you want? If not, then don't worry whether or not someone else has it easier than you do, or that someone else is in a better situation, or has more money, or more contacts. That means nothing to you, because you don't have what they have anyway—you only have what you have. Dreaming about what they have is not a luxury you can indulge in; do not waste your mental energy on it. You need to change your perception about yourself— you must think, "Other people I know have become successful, so I can become successful too."

Life is like a highway with straight sections and curvy sections. Some are uphill and some are downhill. Sometimes you can see around the curve ahead, and sometimes you can't. When you're coming up a hill you can't see what lays on the other side of the hill, whether it is straight or curved, uphill or down hill, steep or flat. All you can do is be prepared for a change and make the best assumptions about what you're going to encounter next. Since you cannot see ahead much of the time because of curves or hills, you can either have a perception that the road ahead will always be difficult to drive, or you could believe that road ahead will be a fun and easy drive. To the road it doesn't matter what you perceive, because it is what it is. However, to you it *does* matter.

Whether you have a perception that the road will be easy or hard to navigate, it will still have the same number of curves and hills in the same places. There are the same number of beautiful meadows and valleys and easy-to-navigate roads in the same places no matter what your perception is. Doesn't it make sense to have a positive view all the time when you are driving since you don't know what's around the curve or over the hill anyway? Won't you make better decisions during the hard times if you're not always stressed out expecting the negative? Most importantly perhaps is the question, won't your drive be more enjoyable if you stay positive?

My point here is there will be a lot of good and not-so-good things that happen to you throughout the rest of your life. Since you don't know when the good or not-so-good things will happen, wouldn't it make more sense to live with a positive perception about life—to believe that life will turn out well for you? This will make you a much happier person. You will be far less stressed out, and because you're not stressed out you will be much better prepared to handle the hard times when they come up. Also, you'll have a better life; isn't that what's best for you, and your loved ones anyway?

Yes, perception is reality; but your reality starts with your perception. Doesn't it make sense to have a perception that always has hope and faith in your ultimate success? Remember, your perception *becomes* your reality. Make your perception of your future a vision of success.

About The Author

Terry Strom

 Terry Strom is a business owner, executive business coach for business owners and CEO's, author, and professional speaker in the areas of motivation, sales, and communication skills. As a professional public speaker, he has spoken in front of over 250,000 business professionals, in small groups, and in arenas with up to 15,000 people in attendance. He is a successful real estate developer and has been the Vice President and Director of three different corporations. Terry has an MBA from USC, is a Certified Guerrilla Marketing Coach, is a Registered Engineer, and is a member of the National Speakers Association.

Terry Strom
Phone: 951.695.0192
Email: terrystrom@thebusinessoptimizer.com
www.thebusinessoptimizer.com

Chapter 2

Les Brown

David E. Wright (Wright)

Today we're talking with Les Brown, an internationally recognized speaker and CEO of Les Brown Enterprises, Inc. He is also the author of the highly acclaimed and successful books, *Live Your Dreams* and the newly released book, *It's Not Over Until You Win.* Les is the former host of the *Les Brown Show,* a nationally syndicated daily television talk show that focused on solutions rather than on problems. Les Brown is one of the nation's leading authorities on understanding and stimulating human potential. Utilizing powerful delivery and newly emerging insights, Les's customized presentations will teach, inspire, and channel any audience to new levels of achievement. Les Brown, welcome to *The Power of Motivation.*

Les Brown (Brown)

Thank you very much. It's a pleasure to be here.

Wright

Les, you've been a role model for thousands of people down through the years because of your triumph over adversity. Tell our readers a little bit about your early life and who was responsible for your upbringing.

Brown

Well, I was born in a poor section of Miami, Florida, called Liberty City. I was born on the floor of an abandoned building along with a twin brother. When we were six weeks of age, we were adopted. When I was in the fifth grade I was identified as EMR (Educable Mental Retarded) and put back into the fourth grade. I failed again when I was in the eighth grade.

I attribute everything that I've accomplished to my mother. I always quote Abraham Lincoln by saying whenever I give a presentation, "All that I am and all that I ever hope to be I owe to my mother." I saw a sign once that said, "God took me out of my biological mother's womb and place me in the heart of my adopted mother." I love my adopted mother's faith, her character, her drive, her dedication, and her willingness to do whatever it took to raise seven children by herself. She only had a third grade education but she had a Ph.D. in mothering.

Wright

If I remember correctly, you were diagnosed at the age of 36 with dyslexia. How did that happen?

Brown

No, I was never diagnosed with dyslexia; but I was in special education from fourth grade all the way through senior high school. My formal education ended at that time; but I became very much interested in personal development tapes and books because of a high school teacher who challenged me to do something in a class. I told him I couldn't do it and he insisted that I could.

Finally, I said, "I can't because I'm Educable Mentally Retarded."

He said, "Don't ever say that again. Someone's opinion of you does not have to become your reality."

This teacher's name was Mr. Leroy Washington and he's still around today. One of the things he emphasized to all of his students was that you don't get in life what you *want*; you get in life what you *are*. What you achieve—what you produce in life—is a reflection of your growth and development as a person. So you must invest in yourself.

He often quoted scripture by saying, "Be ye not conformed to this world be ye transformed by the renewing of your mind" (Romans 12:2). He said most people fail in life because "they don't know that they don't know and they think they know"—they suffer from mental malnutrition. He said take the time each day to develop your mind, read ten to fifteen pages of something positive every day, and find some goals that are beyond your comfort zone that can challenge you to reinvent yourself. He told his students that in order to do something you've never done, you've got to be someone you've never been. He told us the possibilities of what you could achieve by developing your mind and developing your communication skills (because once you open your mouth you tell the world who you are). You can really begin to climb the ladder of success and do things that will literally amaze you.

Wright

So your education is self-education.

Brown

Yes.

Wright

Listening to tapes and reading books and that sort of thing?

Brown

Yes. Going to seminars and then testing and experimenting. I think it's very important people experiment with their lives and find out what it is that works for them—what gives their lives a sense of joy and meaning. What is it that brings music to your life? That way you're able to discover some talents, abilities, and skills you don't even realize you have.

Wright

I remember reading your first book, *Live Your Dreams*. This best-seller is helping people even today. Can you tell us what you're trying to say in this book and why it is important?

Brown

What I'm doing in *Live Your Dreams* is challenging people to look at their situation and ask themselves some crucial questions. Is life working for me? Is it really giving me what I want?

When most people get out of high school, they end up doing things that other people want them to do. Albert Schweitzer was asked a question, "What's wrong with humankind today?" He replied, "Men simply don't think." He meant that statement in a generic sense. Men *and* women simply don't challenge themselves to think about what it is that really makes them happy and gives their life a sense of meaning, purpose, power, and value.

I want to challenge people to think about what it is that really gives their life a sense of meaning and power. Once you determine that, assess yourself. What are your strengths? What are your weaknesses? What is it you bring to the table of life? What help? What assistance? What training? What education? What resources? What do you have to tap into that will help you to become the kind of person that can produce those results?

Then next is to commit yourself. Don't ask yourself, "How am I going to do it? How is none of your business—what is most important is to get started—the how will come. The way will come. Everything you need to attract—the people, the resources, and the assistance—will come to be available at your disposal.

Wright

What do you think about goal setting? There has been so much written about it lately.

Brown

I think it's very important that people set goals because what that does is allow you to focus your energy. It helps you to put together a game plan and a strategy and an agenda for your life. If you don't have an agenda for your life, then you're going to be a part of somebody else's agenda; therefore, you want to set some goals. There's a quote I love very much that says, "People who aim at nothing in life usually hit nothing dead on the head."

Wright

Oh, my.

Brown

Yes, so you want to have some goals you are setting in each area of your life. You want to monitor those goals after you put together a plan of action to achieve those goals. Break those goals down into manageable increments: long-range and short-range goals, three-month goals, thirty-day goals, and weekly goals. You should have daily tasks and activities you engage in that will move you in the direction of your goals. Dr. Robert H. Schuller said something that is true, "By the yard it's hard, but inch by inch anything is a cinch."

As you begin to look at the big picture and come back to where you are right now, looking at the completed big picture of where you want to go, then you can begin to put together a strategy of things and activities you need to do each day to move you in the direction of those goals. As you get closer to those goals you have set for yourself in the various areas of your life—your physical life, your emotional life, your spiritual life, your financial life—then you can begin to push the goals back. Continue to stretch—continue to push yourself—and reach farther.

Wright

A few years ago you had a nationally syndicated television talk show. It's next to impossible to get a show of that nature on the air. Tell us the circumstances that helped to get your show on the air.

Brown

I believe I'm coming back, I don't think it's impossible to get back on again. I wanted to go in a different direction. During the time I ventured into it, television was based upon a formula the executives were accustomed to which they'd always implemented—the show must be based upon conflict and controversy. So you had Phil Donahue, Oprah Winfrey, Sally Jesse Raphael, and Geraldo. My show was based upon solutions. I believed you could have a show that was not based upon conflict and controversy—you could have a show where you would look at what challenges people are facing, who has gone through a challenge and has come out on the other side? Talk to that person and find out how they got there. Interview a guest who is in the middle of a challenge and find one who's just approaching that challenge. Have an expert work them through that process during the hour of the show, asking what is it that brought you here? There's an old saying that goes, "wherever you find yourself, at some point and time, you made an appointment to get there."

The other thing is that success leaves clues. What we must do is talk to someone who's had the same problem you've had and find out from his or her experience what is it you can do to implement a game plan. What help and support will you need to work through this problem?

The Les Brown Show was very successful. It was the highest rated and fastest cancelled talk show in the history of television. It was cancelled because, even though it had successful ratings, the producers of the show wanted me to do a show based upon conflict and controversy and sensationalism—fathers who sleep with their 14-year-old daughter's boyfriends—and subjects like that. I decided to be true to my concept and not venture off into those other areas to do those Jerry Springer type shows, so they cancelled the show and brought someone else in who was willing to cooperate with what they wanted.

Wright

Did you learn any lessons from your highly competitive talk show?

Brown

Yes I did. The lesson I learned was I should have been the executive producer. I was hired talent and, "the hand that pays the piper calls the tune." Had I been the executive producer of my show like Oprah Winfrey, then I could have done what Oprah did after she saw the success of my show—she changed direction and used the formula I'd come up with and the rest is history.

If I had it to do over again I would've put my own production company together, continued to do the show I was doing, and would've found someone else to syndicate the show nationally. If I couldn't find someone to syndicate the show nationally I would've set it up to do it locally and then rolled it back out nationally myself.

Wright

I bet you still get stopped on the street by people who saw your commercials on the PBS station for many years. Those were some of the best produced I've ever seen.

Brown

Well, thank you. We've gotten a lot of response from PBS. We just did one show four months ago called, *It's in Your Hands*. In fact, I end the show with my children because five of my seven children are speakers as well; they're also trainers. What we're doing is teaching people how to become responsible for their careers, their health, and for their family life. The response has been very, very successful on PBS.

Wright

So you're growing your own speakers, then.

Brown

Yes, and I'm training speakers—I'm more of a speech coach. I've developed a reputation as a speaker, but I have a gift of helping people tell their story and to position it so it has value for an audience. I have people's stories create special, magical moments within the context of their presentation so that those stories can create a committed listening audience and move them to new heights within themselves.

Wright

Yes, you don't have to tell me you're a sought after speaker. We were planning a speaking engagement in Ohio and the two people who were requested more than any others were Stephen Covey and Les Brown. They really came after you, so you do have quite a reputation for helping people.

Brown

Thank you.

Wright

A lot of our readers have read many books that advocate focus in their career. I know you've done several things and you've done them well. Do you advocate going in one direction and not diversifying in your career?

Brown

I think that you have to find one area you want to focus on and as you develop momentum in that area and reach a certain measure of success, then you can branch off into other areas.

Wright

Les, you had a serious bout with cancer a few years ago, right?

Brown

Yes.

Wright

How did this catastrophic disease affect your life?

Brown

What cancer did for me was help me live life with a sense of urgency that tomorrow is not guaranteed. It helped me reprioritize my life and find out what's really important. When something major like cancer happens in your life you spend more time focusing on those things. So, even though I always practiced and advocated that people live each day as if it were their last, my cancer battle helped me to focus even more so on priorities. That's what I began to be about the business of doing—thinking about my legacy, spending more time with my children, my grandchildren, and friends who I cared about, and working on the purpose I've embraced for my life.

Wright

My wife was going through cancer at the same time you were, I remember. I heard her say recently that even though she doesn't want cancer again, she wouldn't give anything for the lessons she learned going through it.

Brown

Yes. It helps; it gives new meaning to life, and you value things you used to take for granted.

Wright

So, you did gain a lot of insight into what's important?

Brown

Oh, without any question I did.

Wright

Your new book, *It's Not Over Until You Win*, has been long awaited, of course. Would you tell our readers what it's about and what you're trying to say?

Brown

I think what people must do is challenge themselves to overcome the inner conversation that has been placed in us through our conditioning, through our environment, and our circumstances. We live in a world where we're told more about our limitations rather than our potential. We need to overcome and defeat that conversation.

If you ask most people if they have ever been told they can't achieve a goal that they envision for their life will say, "Yes." My whole goal is to help people learn how to become unstoppable. Yes, it's going to be difficult—it's going to be hard. You're going to have obstacles thrown in your path. You will have setbacks and disappointments. But, you must develop the mind-set of a winner. You must come back again and again and again. You must be creative and flexible, versatile and adaptable, and never stop until you reach your goals.

Wright

I read many years ago that ninety-eight percent of all failure comes from quitting. Would you agree with that?

Brown

Yes, I agree with that without any question. Most people become discouraged and they see delay as a denial. I encourage people to go back to the drawing board in their minds, regroup, and get some fresh thinking. Einstein said, "The thinking that has brought me this far has created some problems that this thinking can't solve."

Sometimes we have to allow other people to be a part of the process—to look at the situation we're battling with new eyes that can help us overcome the challenges we're facing.

Wright

As I have said before, you have been a role model for thousands of adults as well as young people. Do you have any advice to give our readers that would help them to grow in body, mind, and spirit and live a better, fuller life?

Brown

Yes. I think it's important for people to raise the bar on themselves every day. Look at your life and understand and know you are greater than you give yourself credit for being, you have talents and abilities you haven't even begun to reach for yet.

Jim Rohn has a quote I love, "When the end comes for you, let it find you conquering a new mountain, not sliding down an old one." So, therefore, we have to raise the bar on ourselves constantly and assess ourselves.

The other thing is I believe it's important we ask for help, not because we're weak but because we want to remain strong. Many people don't ask for help because of pride. "Pride cometh before a fall" because of ego. Ego means edging God out.

I think that you also have to ask yourself, what is your plan for being here? Most people take their health for granted; but living a long, healthy life is not a given—pain is a given—you have to fight to stay here. You have to have a plan of action to stay here. So what is your plan for being here? Put yourself on your to-do list. Develop a plan of action on how you're going to take better care of yourself and spend more time with people you care about. Focus on living the goals and dreams you've envisioned for yourself that are the calling on your life.

Wright

Down through the years, as you've made your decisions, has faith played an important role in your life?

Brown

Yes, faith is very important. I think you have to believe in yourself, believe in your abilities, believe in your dreams, and believe in a power greater than yourself. There's a quote I love which says, "Faith is the oil that takes the friction out of living." Do the best you can and leave the rest to a power greater than yourself.

Wright

Les, you don't know how much I appreciate you being with us today on *The Power of Motivation*.

Brown

Oh, thank you so much.

Wright

Today we've been talking with Les Brown, an internationally recognized speaker and CEO of Les Brown Enterprises. He's the author of *Live Your Dreams* and *It's Not Over Until You Win*. I suggest you run down to the bookstore and look for both of them. Les has been a successful talk show host and as we have heard today, he is now coaching speakers. Thank you so much for being with us, Les.

Brown

Thank you, I appreciate you very much.

About The Author

Les Brown

Les Brown is an internationally recognized speaker and CEO of Les Brown Enterprises, Inc. He is also the author of the highly acclaimed and successful books, *Live Your Dreams* and *It's Not Over Until You Win.* Les Brown is one of the nation's leading authorities in understanding and stimulating human potential.

Les Brown Enterprises
PO Box 27380
Detroit, Michigan 48227
Phone: 800.733.4226
Email: speak@lesbrown.com
Website: www.lesbrown.com

Chapter 3

Why Be Normal?

Terry Watson

David E. Wright (Wright)

Today we're talking with Terry Watson. Terry is the youngest person ever to be inducted into the Accredited Buyer Representative (ABR®) Hall of Fame for excellence in representing buyers. He is the youngest person ever to be requested by a president of the National Association of Realtors (NAR) to negotiate on behalf of NAR for international disputes and only one of 156 people in the world to be awarded the Distinguished Real Estate Instructor (DREI) designation and the youngest person ever to receive such an award.

Terry has earned the CRS, CRB, CIPS, ABR, ABRM, LTG, GRI, SRES, CFS, DREI, At Home with Diversity—One America, and e-Pro designations.

A class Terry created is required by all new employees at the National Association of Realtors©. From only word-of-mouth with no advertising, Terry has been requested and has spoken in Argentina, Australia, Brazil, Canada, New Zealand, Peru, and all across the United States from Alabama to Alaska with no marketing whatsoever.

Terry is an active, second generation REALTOR© who works for his family's real estate office in Chicago, which he and his mother started over twelve years ago while he was still in college. When Terry started selling real estate, he received no formal training from any real estate franchise or any other real estate office. This forced him to create unorthodox but highly effective techniques. His unorthodox methods are so successful that after hearing him speak, Northwestern University in Chicago asked him to chair their Real Estate Department in the School of Continuing Studies and tweak their real estate courses. He is the youngest person ever to be asked to do so.

He is a resident Generation Xer who believes that education must be entertaining and cutting edge.

Terry, welcome to *The Power of Motavation*.

Terry Watson (Watson)

Thank you, David.

Wright

So, tell me, how do you define "motivation"?

Watson

In my opinion, I would basically define motivation as the ability to do what needs to be done even when you don't feel like doing it.

Wright

So how does it impact our lives?

Watson

There are a lot of things people know that they need to do. I feel that whatever it is you need to do to change your life, the average person already has within himself or herself. People know what it is they need to do and they know exactly how they need to do it; but the problem is they don't have the motivation to do it. And if they had the motivation, they would do it.

Wright

I know that you speak about 180 to 200 days a year, which is a lot in my opinion. So why is this motivation industry such a big business?

Watson

Well, it's something everyone needs. It's like the soap industry—everybody needs to bathe—and everybody needs motivation. It's something that's fleeting. It is something that does not last and because it does not last it needs to be replenished. Everyone gets to a point in their life or a point in their day where don't feel like doing something and they need an extra push to get them to actually move and do it.

I would basically look at motivation as "energy drinks." You look at Red Bull—they've sold more than three billion cans. You look at coffee—people don't get up in the morning, drink coffee and say, "You know what, I want to turn my teeth brown this morning; let me drink some coffee." They drink coffee for that kick and the kick is their motivation. In other words, "I know what I need to—I need the energy to do it." And then they drink coffee to add the impetus to propel them to do whatever it is they need to do. That is what motivation does.

Wright

So at what stage of a person's life, does motivation become critical?

Watson

In my opinion, I'm going to say every stage. If you look at it, even a child, at some level, has to be motivated to eat their peas. No child gets up in the morning looking to eat strained peas or strained carrots—you have motivated them to do it and you can find all types of ways. Even from early childhood experiences you have to find some way to get people to do things even when they don't want to do it.

Wright

Would you explain to our readers the relationship between motivation and success?

Watson

I think it's a direct relationship. For a lot of people, there are things that should be done, but are not done because there's no motivation. In my opinion there are three main reasons why a lot of people not motivated: The main one, in my opinion, is energy. If someone doesn't have energy, they're not going to do the things they know they should do.

I have a friend right now who has two children. She wants three so bad it hurts, but she's always saying, "I just don't have the energy to do it." If a person doesn't have the energy the person is not going to be motivated.

I wake up in the morning and there are things I need to do. If I don't have the energy, I'm not going to do it.

And many people aren't motivated. You go to your computer, you turn it on and you see 3,000 e-mails waiting for you and you know there are important e-mails you need answer but you're exhausted. You want to do it, you know you need to do it, but you don't have the energy to do it, nor the motivation, so you don't do it.

Wright

So what published authors have motivated you to become successful?

Watson

I'm going to say several. One of my favorite authors I think everyone should read is Coach John Wooden. I think the guy is absolutely a genius in what he does. He is one of the most centered people I've ever read. The thing I like about him is he's a master at motivating people. His record in basketball is unparalleled, even to this day. He basically takes people from different groups, who each have a different character, different backgrounds, and finds out what specifically motivates them. In his book he says some people you can motivate with fear, some people you can't—the stick does not always work—you have to find something else. But anything by John Wooden I absolutely love.

Another book that is one of my absolute favorites and that I feel truly affects motivation is about your environment. Many people don't realize that you feed off your environment—good, bad, or indifferent. One of my favorite books and one of my favorite authors is Karen Kingston. Her book, *Clear Your Clutter with Feng Shui,* explains how to clean up your environment and when you clean up your environment you're at peace. If I sit in my office and I have paper everywhere (I should have a "no smoking" sign because there's so much paper), it brings me down. One of my favorite quotes is from the Dalai Lama and it simply says that your external surroundings mirror your internal thoughts. If you have chaos around you, you're going to have chaos inside of you and that will affect your ability to do anything; and it will have a dramatic affect on your motivation.

Wright

So what impact do role models have on motivation?

Watson

I think it's something you can't even begin to measure, and here's why: One of the motivational mistakes people make is they don't surround themselves with people who will encourage them to be who they really are and encourage them to do more than they're doing. Also, many people do not surround themselves with people will tell them the truth. I want people around me who will tell me i.e., "The baby is ugly." These are the kinds of people I want around me, who will tell me exactly what I need to hear whether I want to hear it or not.

Another motivational mistake is that many people do not associate with people who shatter their reality of what's possible. That is what good role models do for people.

For example, I thought the most real estate anyone could sell within a year is 600 homes until I talked with someone who sells 1,000 homes. Now my 600 ceiling is blown out of the water. Now I've realized that with systems and assistants you can double or even triple your production. It's like Roger Bannister with the four-minute mile—once he did it, everyone else realized it was possible; but many people do not associate with people who alter their concept of reality by showing them they are capable of doing so much more. If you can't associate with them, listen to them, read their books, and watch their videos. They will show you it's possible and then you can deny all the other people who believe it's not possible.

Anytime someone is diagnosed with cancer or some other kind of disabling disease, it's critical for him or her to talk with someone who has beaten it. Many doctors will tell you it's not possible, your disease is incurable, etc. It's critical for them to listen to someone who will say, "That is what I was told and I'm still standing."

Wright

A few minutes ago you said that motivation impacts our energy levels. How does that happen?

Watson

Energy and motivation are intermarried—if there's a problem with one, you have a problem with the other. One of the biggest mistakes I see people make is with their environment. I believe one of the most important parts of your day is the first thirty minutes after you get up. The average person reads the newspaper or they watch the news. In my opinion, the news is just like watching a soap opera. If you do not watch the soap opera and you go back to it one, two, or three years later, it's the same story with different people.

If you don't watch news or you go to another country where there's no television and you come back and watch the news a year later, someone was murdered, some high profile person is dating another high profile person, some high profile person had an affair, someone was molested, the economy is going up, the economy is going down, real estate is going up, real estate is going down, the stock market is going up, the stock market is going down. Well, that doesn't help you.

In my opinion, the first thirty minutes after you wake up, your brain is the most active. I cannot tell you how many times when I've first awakened and heard something on the radio that was some stupid jingle, just totally stupid, I didn't like it, or some song that had nothing to do with me, I basically had that song or jingle in my mind all day long.

What I tell people they should do, in my opinion, regarding motivation is this: as soon as I get up the first thing in the morning I listen to something positive. I do not listen to the news, I do not listen to the weather; I listen to something positive every single morning.

One of the most wasted spaces in the house, in my opinion, is the bathroom. In my bathroom I have speakers in my shower so as I'm showering I'm listening to something motivational—something to keep me up. Most people are just sitting there looking down, looking at the wall, and talking to themselves. The bathroom is my "reprogram chamber." I sit there and I listen to something positive.

One of my favorite tapes I'm listening to now and I listen to it every single morning is Mark Victor Hansen's *The Success Principles*. I listen to that every single day when I first get up. The first thirty minutes are absolutely critical.

Another thing is I do a lot of research on is sleep studies. What most people agree is that for your body to heal itself, it will only happen while you're sleeping. Certain functions will not happen unless you're sleeping. The average person does not sleep enough. What many sleep studies experts totally agree on is that, if at all possible, you need to be in bed by 10 P.M. and you need to be up by 6 A.M. If you stay in bed beyond 6 A.M. you're not doing your body much good. In fact, many studies I read will basically state that if you're in bed after 6 A.M. you start losing energy. If I stay in bed beyond 7 P.M. my back hurts and I wake up tired.

People want to start their day and they have all these things they want to do but they have no energy, and they're not motivated *because* they have no energy.

Wright

Let's bottom-line you specifically. What keeps *you* motivated?

Watson

I'm going to say what keeps me motivated are several things:

1. I associate with people who basically force me to be who I really am. I've spent so much time reading and listening to tapes. If you open the glove box in my car it's almost pathetic—tapes and CDs fall out.

For example, I was at an airport the other day. The backpack I travel with weighs at least fifty pounds—when I put in my laptop, my projector, and everything, it weighs a minimum of fifty pounds. At some airports you can walk a mile or two between gates. At Dallas, for example, you're always running for a flight—it's exhausting. I had three connections that day and I was literally exhausted. I bought a DVD about Navy Seals. I popped that into my computer and I watched it. I was tired, I was feeling sorry for myself, my legs hurt, and my back hurt. On the DVD I saw that they had those guys on beaches carrying telephone poles. When I saw that, suddenly I was fiercely motivated. I told myself I had to, "soldier up, I'm being a baby!" Telephone poles and I'm concerned about a fifty-pound backpack! All of a sudden I felt great again. On my next flight I was good to go but I just basically flood my brain with positive things and things that keep me motivated and people who are doing it.

One of my favorite things to watch on television are biographies. I'm always watching the *True Hollywood Stories* program where they show how successful people are and what they went through to get there. Once you see that, you don't feel bad at going through whatever it is you're going through—you realize it's just part of the process. People take their own problems and think, "This is happening to me, this is horrible." It's just a process and if you realize other people go through the process it doesn't bother you all—it becomes relative.

Wright

When you're talking and sharing with your audiences, I know you cover three main motivational secrets. Would you share them with our readers and perhaps tell us why they're important?

Watson

One motivational secret that I try to get across is what I call the "ninety-eight percent rule." It is simply: Two percent of the people in your life will cause you ninety-eight percent of the grief you will experience. I totally agree with that. What I tell people in class is they need to make a list of the names of those people in that two percent and they need to dump them.

Every year I make a list of all the people I have in my life—everyone—anybody who I associate with and talk with again and again—I make a list twice a year. I look at the list and if on some level they're not contributing to my life, they get cut. You can do that all by yourself. I read in a book somewhere the statement, "Everyone is either a motor or an anchor—they're just speeding you up or pulling you down." And too many people have all these anchors in their lives; if they just drop the dead weight they'd be better off.

Look at any racecar. They only put on a racecar what is needed to get it to the finish line. If it's dead weight it's stripped. You don't need a back seat in a racecar—gone. You don't need a heater—gone. They only put in what is needed.

I cannot tell you how many times I've evaluated my list and said, "This person is not supportive." I believe the criteria should not only include whether or not a person is supportive but whether or not the person has good energy or bad energy. Bad energy is what sucks the motivation out of someone's soul like a straw. Bad energy is when you see someone's name on caller I.D. you don't pick up. There's good energy and when you meet some people and you feel good just talking with them, you listen to their story, you feel great, and you're motivated, you keep that person in your life. So for me the ninety-eight percent rule is critical.

The next thing I think is absolutely important is this: Most people don't look at their life as a business. I am starting to make huge changes. I look at my life like a business and I am the CEO of my business. The major mistake that most people make is they have no formal written business plan. The average person in this country does not have a business plan. If I went to a bank today and told them I want to start a new business, I guarantee you—unless we have some serious personal relationship—they're going to say, "I want to see your financials and I want to see your business plan." Most people have no plan whatsoever.

One of my favorite books I read at least once every six months is the *E-Myth Revisited* by Michael E. Gerber. He talks about why most businesses fail. If you look at your life as a business, it makes total sense.

A major motivational mistake most people make is they don't have systems. An important innovation in my life now is anything I do more than three times, I need to have a system for. Gerber talks about McDonald's—the most successful restaurant in the world—run by sixteen-year-olds who can't even clean up their bedrooms. But the restaurant is successful because they have a system.

If I find myself doing a task again and again I ask myself how I can make a system for it. For example, I used to wake up every morning and every single morning I wouldn't be able to find my keys. I thought about it and then went to Home Depot. I bought a package of finishing nails, went to my closet with those nails and a spoon— because I couldn't find a hammer either—and I nailed a finishing nail into my wall. As soon as I come in I take my keys and hang them on the finishing nail. As medieval and as barbaric as that sounds, I've never lost my keys since then—ever.

There's another thing I did that made a huge difference. I buy a lot of technology and because I buy a lot of technology, a lot of it doesn't work. When I take it back to the store I could never find the receipt. The store would give me a store credit instead of a refund because I couldn't produce the receipt. Now, anytime I buy something I tape the receipt to the bottom of whatever it is I buy. If you take my television and turn it upside down, the receipt is taped to the bottom. If you take my telephone, the receipt is taped to the bottom. You cannot believe what that's done for me; but it's a system. Whatever it is that you're doing more than three times, you need to have a system for it.

The third thing I think that is absolutely critical is visualizing things. If you talk with any Olympic athlete they will tell you that they picture exactly what it is they want to have happen. They see it again, and again, and again. The average person is visual. If you ask the average person, "When you assemble something, do you read the instructions or do you just look at the picture and figure it out?" They'll tell you they look at the picture and they try and figure it out (that's why there always seems to be the extra pieces left over).

If you go to my bathroom and look at my shower, you will see pictures of all the things that I want. It has never failed me. I'll look at the picture, I'll keep seeing it, and keep seeing it, and suddenly I'll meet someone who will tell me about something like what's in the picture I've been looking at or someone who knows someone, or someone who wants to help me.

Right now, one of my physical goals is I want to get a set of six-pack abs. I may have a one-pack right now but I want a six-pack. What I did was I went to the store and bought a bunch of Calvin Klein underwear. On the packages of Calvin Klein underwear, all the models have six-pack abs. I took probably about five of the pictures of models from the packages of my new Calvin Klein underwear, cut their heads off, took my business card which has my picture on it, took my head and planted my head on top of the pictures of their bodies. So if you go to my shower right now, there are six pictures of Calvin Klein models with my head on their bodies. As I'm showering I'm looking at those pictures thinking, "This is who I will be, this is who I will be." Whatever it is that you want you have to visualize it.

Regarding the last four cars I purchased, I went to the dealer, I took a photo of the car and I put it on my wall. I would look at it and then just by whatever means necessary, without effort, within three to six months I've always had that car. Just something happened; but you've got to picture it.

The fourth thing I would like to add that I tell people that is critical is about money. One of the things that will totally drain your motivation is finances. The average person never gets control of their finances. I tell people, "If you want to affect your motivation, one of the most important things you can ever do for you for your family is get a debt elimination plan, immediately."

At one point I had probably close to, or a little more than, one hundred thousand dollars in credit card debt. When my grandmother was dying I took off for nine months and stayed in the hospital with her and lived off my credit cards. I racked up an unbelievable amount of debt. American Express with Citibank came after Generation Xers, people like me—like pit bulls, when we were in college. In the bookstore I got credit card applications. The average person is probably one or two checks away from financial humility.

What I suggest for people to do like yesterday, is to get on some kind of debt elimination plan. I am now completely debt free except for twelve thousand dollars I owe on a car. You have no idea the financial freedom you have when you go to the mailbox and you're not taking out a stack of bills. I remember at one point I would just sit there and look at them and not even open them. Just opening them I could feel my blood pressure going up. I could feel a vein popping out and starting to throb just looking at all those bills.

Many marriages, many relationships break up because of finances. If the finances together you're motivated to do something else. But if you're worried about if you're going to eat, or if your furniture is going to get put out on the street, that's going to affect everything. You can't think, "Let's go out and save the planet," after something like that.

Finances, in my opinion, are absolutely critical.

Wright

When you're talking about the main motivational secrets, may I ask you what the antithesis of that is? What are the top three motivational mistakes made by ninety-nine percent of the people?

Watson

1. Not asking for help. In my opinion, no one can do things long-term on the level they are capable of doing them without help. Everyone needs help. If you look at any truly successful person they' have had help. For example, any president who has ever occupied the Whitehouse has had a Cabinet. That Cabinet's job was to help them. When you read the Bible you see that Jesus had disciples. Everybody has someone they need who could help them. I think this is absolutely critical. The average person doesn't believe in relying on others to help.

2. Being a perfectionist—perfectionism.

Not asking for help and perfectionism, in my opinion, go hand-in-hand. During the majority of my life I did everything myself and it had to absolutely be perfect. One reason I didn't ask for help is I didn't think anyone could do it as good as I could. And I wanted it to be done just my perfect way.

Think about this. Perfectionism is a curse to people who want everything to be perfect and it totally holds you back. And it does stop you from motivation. You get motivated as you continue. Small, incremental successes start to motivate you.

When a boxer is being trained to be a world champion, trainers don't start them out fighting world champions. They start out having them compete with people they know are beatable. They let them get successes under their belt winning fights with fighters who are beatable. Their self-esteem goes up, they start to feel good, and they get momentum. Movement creates momentum.

What I tell people now in class is, "You need to be like Bill Gates." Bill Gates is arguably one of, if not the richest man in the world. Does he wait until Windows is absolutely perfect before he puts it in the marketplace? Of course not. He takes it and he keeps making it better.

One of my favorite quotes is, "Never let perfection stand in the way of better." You just keep making it better and as you keep making it better you gain momentum. As you gain momentum you're getting energy, if you're getting energy, that's going to keep you motivated.

1. The third major mistake people make is they don't make a public declaration. If you make a public declaration, many times, even if you don't have the energy, even if you're not motivated, because of the fear of being disgraced you will do what needs to be done.

For example, if you have a son and you say, "Friday night I'm coming to your ballgame," I don't care if you stayed up all night working on a project Thursday and you look like an albino hamster, because you know it would break his heart, you're going to do whatever it takes to be there. What got you there was a public declaration. Many people will do more for someone else than they'll do for themselves. If you talk to any mother, you'll find that's true.

Wright

This is an interesting conversation. I would like to ask one more question that I think is very important to this conversation. In your opinion, why do so many people with above average talent and ability in life live a life of "quiet desperation"?

Watson

I would say, in my opinion, the reason that this is so is because of the major mistake many people make of not surrounding themselves with people who force them to be more than they are. That is the major reason.

For example, I want to go out and I want to purchase property. I want to be the largest individual owner of apartments in all of Chicago. I've had that dream since I first saw Wall Street years and years ago. The problem was the dream was just inside of me. Now I've associated myself with people who own fifty apartments, 100, 200 and 300 apartments. Now there's so much pressure on me to meet my goal. I just went out and bought a four-unit building. My goal is to buy twenty or thirty units every year because I feel like something is wrong with me for not meeting the standards of those I'm associating with. When I see others who are not more intelligent, not more gifted, did not have better opportunities, and they're accomplishing this goal, I really have no excuse.

The other major reason why people who live a life of total desperation is fear. They flat out don't do it because they're scared. Many people have a fear of failure, many people have a fear of success, and many people are waiting for everything to be perfect. But the major thing is fear—fear of the unknown. They're afraid that if they go out there, what's going to happen if they change, and/or what's going to happen if they fail?

The easiest way, in my opinion, to overcome these fears is to surround yourself with people who have already done what it is you need to do. What I tell people in class is, "You need to find someone successful and you have to get next to them and find out what they know. You have to get the information, figure out what it is that they're doing." If I'm around anyone for three minutes I start asking him or her questions. It almost seems like an interrogation. I have a billion questions because I have a deep desire and need to know what it is they're doing right. One little piece of information can change your life—just one.

Another major reason why people live lives of desperation is because they don't take action. They get the information but they don't act upon it. I have a friend, Jack, who basically gave me the following metaphor:

He said, "Terry, there are four frogs sitting on a log. One decides to jump off. How many are left?"

"Three," I replied.

"No, four. All it did was decide," he said.

You have to take action—you have to do something. Many people don't do that something—they just listen, gather information but never take action.

I would say the last reason why people live lives of quiet desperation is they're not committed. I have a friend right now who I have been trying to get to purchase real estate for the last two years. She knows she should purchase real estate. She says she wants to purchase real estate, but she's not committed. She dabbles—she is nowhere near being committed. She's not saying, "This will happen no matter what." One of the reasons she's not committed is she will not make a public declaration. She won't tell anyone because she would be embarrassed if she didn't follow through. She won't tell her boss, she won't tell her son, she won't tell other people because she's very concerned about what others think about her, so she won't tell them she will do this by this date—it will happen. She'll be embarrassed if it doesn't happen. You'd be absolutely amazed at the internal pressure making a public declaration will put on you to accomplish something even when you don't want to do it.

Wright

Well, what a great conversation, Terry. I really appreciate your taking all this time with me this morning here talking about this powerful thing called motivation. Thank you so much for being with us and for sharing all this information.

Watson

I appreciate your having me.

Wright

Today we've been talking with Terry Watson who is an active REALTOR©. He is most of all, in my opinion, a teacher and a trainer for corporate work. He has spoken and has earned rave reviews in places like Argentina, Australia, Brazil, Canada, New Zealand, Peru, and of course all across his own country from Alabama to Alaska.

Terry, thank you so much for being with us today on *Power of Motivation*.

About The Author

Terry Watson

Terry has his own unique brand of imparting knowledge. His infectious can-do attitude, his joyous sense of humor, and his uncanny ability to reach and involve all types of learners makes him and his seminar memorable and useful. He is doing something amazing at each event. That's why it's no surprise that Terry is quickly becoming one of the most sought after trainers in North America. Today, Terry is a broker for his family's real estate firm, where he has hired, trained, and supervised over 100 REALTOR® professionals. After selling for franchises while in high school, Terry reached the status of "top" salesperson before age 25. He also is founder and president of Watson World, Inc.©, a thriving consulting firm for which he delivers keynote speeches, offers motivational seminars, and provides educational training. This business has allowed him to travel to and work in Brazil, Costa Rica, Mexico, Argentina, Australia, Canada, New Zealand, Peru and throughout North America from Alabama to Alaska. No matter what Terry does, he puts all of his energy into it and truly cares about the outcome. This is probably why he is the youngest person ever to be inducted into the Accredited Buyer Representative (ABR®) Hall of Fame. He also is one of only 156 people in the world to hold the Distinguished Real Estate Instructor (DREI) designation and so far is the youngest person ever to be named as such. Terry is as devoted to self-improvement as he is to helping others learn, and his own educational efforts have resulted in him earning the CRS, CRB, CIPS, ABR, ABRM, LTG, GRI, SRES, CFS, DREI, At Home with Diversity - One America, and e-Pro designations. Don't you want to hear what Terry has to say, too, then walk away smiling?

Terry Watson, International Speaker
WATSON WORLD, INC.
Bus Add: 1341 W. Fullerton Ave., #303
Chicago, IL 60614
Email: Terry@TerryWatson.com
Fax: 773-880-6550
Bus Tel: 773-404-7721
Web Address: TerryWatson.com

Chapter 4

Get Motivated! Keep Moving!
Be a Success!

Donna Satchell

THE INTERVIEW

David E. Wright (Wright)

Today we are talking with Donna Satchell. She is a professional speaker, trainer, author, and president of STARR Consulting & Training. Her business specializes in helping businesses better serve their customers, helping business teams work better together, and helping individuals achieve remarkable success. She conducts training programs in the areas of customer service, team building, public speaking, and a variety of business topics. She provides motivational speeches inspiring audiences to live more rewarding, fulfilling, and successful lives. Donna believes that "True success comes from reaching beyond one's grasp. It comes from reaching for the stars."

Donna, welcome to *The Power of Motivation*!

Donna Satchell (Satchell)

It is my pleasure. Thank you for inviting me to be in this book.

Wright

Every time I ask this question I get a different answer, depending on whom I ask. How would you describe or define motivation?

Satchell

That is a good question and I have been thinking about it in anticipation of this interview. I would describe motivation as the force or condition that makes people move mentally or physically. It can make people move forward or, sadly, it can make them move backwards. There are many things that motivate people. As I am sure you will agree, for many people, money is a motivator. The need for a change can be a motivator. Love or the lack of love can be motivators. So is being fired, laid off, getting married, and going through a divorce. It can also be the desire to achieve more.

Wright

What are some of the things that you were motivated to pursue?

Satchell

There have been so many. The first that comes to mind was my being motivated to move beyond the administrative support role. I had been a secretary and administrative assistant for a number of years and I wanted to do something different. I wanted a job with greater responsibilities and a higher salary. Those desires lead me to go to college when I was thirty-three years old. Then I wanted to move to Atlanta so I could live in a new city, make new friends and have a different lifestyle. I was motivated to find out what were my gifts and talents; what could I be passionate about doing.

Wright

What do you think keeps people from being motivated?

Satchell

The major thing is negative self-talk. I know that is what kept me from moving forward on my goals and dreams for many years. It is the inner conversations we have with ourselves when we think we cannot do something and we have not put forth the effort. It keeps us stuck and unable to move forward.

I have identified three types of negative self-talk. The first one is what I call the "outer positive" because it starts outside ourselves. Someone says something positive about us. It could be a compliment, praise, or congratulations that we have done a great job and then we turn it around and make it a negative. In our minds, we say it can't be true, they don't know what they're talking about, or they don't have enough experience or knowledge to make that judgment. I think we have all done that from time to time.

Wright

Can you give me an example?

Satchell

A couple of years ago I gave one of my first presentations to a group of 200 administrative assistants. When I was finished, several people told me I had given a great speech. I remember one woman in particular said to me, "You did a fabulous job. You are an excellent speaker. Based on what you said I am going back to college. You have truly inspired me." I smiled, nodded my head and thanked her. However, in my mind I was thinking, "I bet she has never heard outstanding speakers, like Zig Ziglar, Tony Robbins or Les Brown." Those are speakers I had admired for years. She had complimented me; yet I made her compliment less valid by thinking that she had not heard speakers I considered excellent. That is an example of being told something positive and then turning it around to be less positive than it was intended.

Wright

That is interesting. What are the other types?

Satchell

The next I call the "outer negative." Someone says something to us that is negative. They express their disapproval of something we have done or are thinking about doing and we immediately think it is true. We do not even consider getting someone else's opinion, or thinking it over in our own minds.

Wright

Can you give me an example?

Satchell

About a year ago I was having lunch with another speaker. I asked her how she started writing articles. She relayed the following story to me. She had written her first article and gave it to another speaker to critique. He told her the article was not well written and she should spend her time developing her speaking skills. Discouraged she put the article in a folder, filed it, and thought to herself that she had no writing skills.

Several months later, someone was helping her clean out her cabinets and they came across the folder and the article. They encouraged her to submit it to a magazine. With much reluctance she decided to do so. You have probably already guessed what happened. She got a reply from the magazine saying it was a good article and they published it. If that were the end, it would be a great story. However, there is more. After it was published, the person who originally said it was not a good article saw her and excitingly exclaimed, "Recently I read an article you wrote. It was excellent!" Apparently he did not remember reading it a year earlier.

I asked her, "Do you think he intentionally discouraged you?"

She said, "No, he is a very supportive person." She further remarked, "Donna, both times he read the article he gave me his opinion. It is just that his opinion had changed." The first time he told her what he thought and she decided not to move forward based on his opinion. However, she never thought to ask someone else or move forward despite his comment. She just thought he must be right.

Wright

That is amazing! Did you say there is a third type?

Satchell

Yes, I call it the "inner dialogue." That is when we tell ourselves we cannot do something because of our age, shortage of money, lack of resources or any other excuse we can think of. We say there is not enough of me, M-E-E-E. I don't have enough money. I don't have enough education. I don't have enough experience. I don't have enough exposure. I don't know the right people and the right people don't know me. And because of the negative inner dialogue we do not move forward on our goals and dreams.

Wright

Do you think that we can overcome negative self-talk?

Satchell

Yes I think we can. But we must be willing to change the way we think.

Wright

How can we do that?

Satchell

I always recommend a technique I read about in the *One Minute Millionaire* by Robert Allen and Mark Victor Hansen. They write about negative self-talk as being a habit—it is a habit we have gotten into. The same way we get into other habits such as spending money unnecessarily, watching lots of television, gossiping about events at the office, or any of the many things we unconsciously do over and over again.

To break the negative self-talk habit they recommend you wear a rubber band around your wrist for a minimum of twenty-one days. Every time you hear yourself thinking or saying something negative, you pull the rubber band so that it pops against your skin. Now you do not pop it so you cause a bruise or damage to your wrist. You pop it slightly to remind yourself of how often you are saying something negative that is holding you back from being motivated to move forward.

You do the exercise for a minimum of twenty-one days because it takes that long to start to change a negative habit. When you hear that negative self-talk, you replace it with a positive affirmation that you are smart enough, young enough, have enough money or resources to get started.

Wright

So once a person becomes more positive, are they motivated?

Satchell

Not necessarily, they are two different things. Being positive sets the stage for motivation because it is hard to be negative and be motivated to move forward. One precedes the other.

Wright

So once someone is positive, how do they move forward on their wishes and wants?

Satchell

They need to know what they want. It is interesting how often I meet people who say they are unhappy because they want something more out of life, but they do not know what. They do not really know what their gifts and talents are. They do not know what they are passionate about.

Wright

So does everyone have a passion to pursue?

Satchell

I believe everyone has the potential of having a passion to pursue. Many people are born with talents and abilities they recognize early in life or that someone else recognized in them at an early age. They are fortunate. I think about people like Paula Abdul who started dancing at a young age. Tiger Woods had a skill for playing golf extremely well as a little boy. Venus and Serena Williams exhibited extraordinary tennis skills as young girls. Those are just a few of the many examples.

Then there are others, like myself, who must search for it. As you know, speaking and training is my passion. However, that was not always the case. For years I would sit in audiences while speakers announced that everyone had special talents and we should be working to express them. I would feel discouraged because I did not know mine. I believe many people are like I was at that period in my life. I was struggling to understand if I had any unique skills and abilities. And for a long time, I thought I did not. That is because, for many years, I had not exposed myself to all of the things that I could do.

Wright

Why was that?

Satchell

I think many times we live in a box, so to speak, and we do not think in terms of all the things we could be doing. I know that was true of me. I stayed with a few activities that I enjoyed doing and did not venture out and try other things. Doing something new and different can expose us to something we could be passionate about or be very good doing.

There is an ad I saw on a billboard the other day and it read, "When was the last time you did something for the first time?" So I ask the readers of this book, "When is the last time you tried something you have never done before?" For people who do not know what they are passionate about, I always recommend that "they get passionate about finding their passion"—make it one of their life's goals to find out.

Wright

How can they find out?

Satchell

First they need to avoid thinking, "I have no special gifts or talents." That negative self-talk can be standing in their way. They need to be positive, persistent and creative. Below are some things they can consider:

- *Doing things you have never done before.* This is the most important one. Make it a goal that every couple of weeks you are doing something new. It could be taking art classes, French cooking, a language class, going to museums, traveling to a place you have not considered before, or, in my case, taking public speaking classes. Whatever it is, just start trying different things until something clicks. In addition, as you're trying new things, notice if anyone says something to you about how good you are in that particular area.

- *Taking on a leadership role* in an organization of which you are member.

- *Considering suggestions from others.* What have you been told that you do exceptionally well?

- *Revisiting your childhood.* Ask yourself, "As a child what did I like doing, love doing, dream about doing? What did others say about me?"

- *Spending time with people who have found their passion.* That can energize you to find yours.

- *Sitting in a kindergarten classroom.* What are you drawn to?

- *Spending quiet time by yourself.* Let your mind wander; where does it take you?

Wright

Is there anything else they can do?

Satchell

They can do a personal inventory of themselves by asking the following questions:

1. What are my strengths?
2. What am I good at doing?
3. What interests me and I enjoy doing?
4. What are my values?
5. What is important to me?

It may take some time to answer these questions; but in the end it is well worth the time invested.

Wright

Once you figure out what you want, then what is next?

Satchell

Next is writing down some goals. Many times if we do not take time to write our goals, nothing happens. Research after research has shown that people who have goals achieve more than people who do not. And people with written goals are much more likely to accomplish them than those with unwritten goals. One of my favorite speakers, Les Brown says, "Don't just think it, you have got to ink it." You have got to write it down.

The SMART system for goal setting is used in many businesses and organizations. SMART is an acronym for the elements required in *writing* goals. I added an E and R to create SMARTER™ because those two letters represent keys to *achieving* goals.

S = Specific
M = Measurable and meaningful
A = Achievable
R = Relates to your future
T = Time-based
E = Energize your goals with action and enthusiasm
R = Review your goals periodically

Specific

Your goals have got to be clear and precise.

Measurable and Meaningful

Measurable means you need to be able to know when you are close to accomplishing your goal or far from it. Your goal should also be something that is meaningful to you; otherwise you are going to lose interest in it. You will not be persistent in pursuing it or doing the work necessary to achieve it.

Achievable

It has to be something that you can actually achieve—not a "pie-in-the-sky" idea.

Relates To Your Future

Does what you are attempting to do move you in the direction of where you want to be in five, ten, or fifteen years? If not, you should reconsider whether it is truly a goal or a distraction.

Time Based

When are you going to start working toward the goal? When are you going to review your progress? When do you plan on completing the goal? I believe the answers to these questions are major keys to goal-setting. I always tell my audiences that at age twenty-seven I said to myself I am going to go to college. I should have gone when I graduated from high schools like all my friends did. But I am going to go to college *someday*.

Do you know what happens with those "someday goals"? Many times the answer is "not a lot." At age twenty-nine I was still thinking about going to college. At thirty-two, I was upset and frustrated with myself because I had not gotten started yet. Finally at age thirty-three I said, "I am going to be in college by the fall." I did not know where I was going to go or how I was going to pay for it. But I wrote it down as a goal with the start date being September. That was the year I finally went to college.

Six years later I graduated with top honors and awards. At that time, I was promoted into a management level marketing position—one of my dreams and motivators for going to college. From that experience, I learned the importance of writing goals and having a timeframe for them.

Energize Your Goals With Action & Enthusiasm

Until you act on your goals they are just ideas waiting to happen. You must put forth the effort needed. And do it with enthusiasm. One of my favorite quotes is, "Nothing great happens without enthusiasm," by Ralph Waldo Emerson. The quote does not say that nothing happens; but rather nothing *great* happens. So if you want to be motivated to achieve great things, you must be enthused and excited about your goals.

Review

Periodically review your goals. You will have to figure out what is working and what is not working. When we review our goals, we can decide between four courses of action:

1. *Repeat.* We keep moving forward because things are going as we planned.
2. *Rearrange.* This means we may have to rearrange some things in our lives so that we can continue to pursue our goals. Sometimes we want to move forward but there are things preventing us from doing so or they are slowing down our progress.
3. *Rewrite.* We might have to rewrite the goals because of some unforeseen circumstances that have surfaced. Or may we have set the bar too high or too low.
4. *Release.* We may find that we no longer want to pursue the goal. Maybe we have lost interest, or circumstances in our lives have changed so drastically that we must put the goal on hold indefinitely. It is all right to re-lease a goal once you have given it a sincere effort. Sometimes we start off wanting to do certain things in life and at some point we realize we no longer desire those things.

Wright

So once you start pursuing your goals, is anything else necessary to stay motivated?

Satchell

In order to stay motivated, you need to have the right people in your life to keep you focused. If you have people who are negative or who are saying negative things to you, that can hold you back. One of my favorite speakers, Jewel Diamond Taylor, says, "Not everyone is healthy enough to have a front row seat in your life."

Wright

That is a very profound statement. Please elaborate on it.

Satchell

At some point you should ask yourself who is occupying your time and what are they contributing to your life? Is what they are contributing positive or negative? Are they moving you forward or holding you back?

Wright

How can someone make those determinations?

Wright

They can make those determinations by asking themselves key questions about people they associate with most often. The questions are:

1. Is this person a positive person? Someone who is negative will eventually have a negative impact on you.

2. Does this person have dreams and goals of their own? When people do not have goals and dreams of their own, they may not understand why and how you can accomplish your goals. They are less likely to be supportive of you.

3. Do they ask specific questions about your goals and dreams? Many times we are talking to people about things we want to accomplish and they are not listening to us. We know that because when we talk to them they do not ask us any specific questions. They simply say things like "So how's everything going?" They do not ask about things you mentioned during previous conversations, like a test you took in college, a business deal you are trying to close, an interview you had for a promotion, or anything connected with your goals and dreams. They do not ask you because they are not interested or are preoccupied with their own concerns.

4. How do they treat other people? Regardless of how well someone behaves towards me, I am uncomfortable when they treat others poorly. Through a costly experience, I learned to be aware of how friends and business colleagues interact with other people. It can be an indication of how they will eventually treat you.

Wright

So once we make the changes needed to keep good people in our lives, is there anything else we need to do to stay motivated?

Satchell

Yes, celebration and self-celebration.

Wright

I understand celebration. But what do you mean by self-celebration?

Satchell

Self-celebration is when we commemorate the things we have achieved without waiting for someone else to recognize our accomplishments in some way. It is not sitting around and hoping for someone else to say, "great job," or, "Congratulations, you were excellent!" It is being willing to look at our own successes and appreciate the things we have done well.

Wright

How do we do that?

Satchell

Self-celebration may be buying yourself something special because you have accomplished a meaningful goal. It could be taking friends out to dinner, as opposed to waiting for them to take you out to dinner. Maybe it is treating yourself to a day at the spa or buying yourself a new golf club. It is doing something to acknowledge your good work.

In our world today, many times our successes can easily go unnoticed for many reasons. It could be that family, friends, and colleagues are so busy that they do not have the time to celebrate with us. Or maybe they do not think that what we accomplished was such a big deal. It could be that they are jealous or envious of us. Or maybe they have issues that are occupying their time, energy, and focus. If we are relying on other people to always celebrate our success, we might end up being very disappointed. I think that, "Self-celebration can lead to self-motivation to do even greater things."

Wright

That is a powerful statement. Could you repeat that?

Satchell

Self-celebration can lead to self-motivation to do even greater things. It opens you up to thinking of all the other things you could be doing in life.

I recommend at the end of each day that people ask themselves three questions:

1. What did I do well today? Not what my manager said I did well, not what my husband, wife, kids, or significant others thought I did well. But rather what do *I* know that I did well today?
2. What could I have done differently today? That reminds us of all the choices we make every day.
3. What am I going to do with what I learned about myself today?

The answers to these questions can help us stay motivated.

Wright

Donna, you talked about defeating negative self-talk, setting goals, evaluating people in our lives, and finding and pursuing our passions. Is there anything else you would like to add that could help our readers stay motivated?

Satchell

I would like to express one last thought and that is understand your purpose. Once we understand the contributions we can make to others, I believe we can stay motivated. Many times, we are so busy we do not fully understand the purposefulness of our activities. We do not connect them to something greater than ourselves. Once we start doing that, then I believe we can be truly motivated. I love the quote by Friedrich Nietzsche, "He who has a why can endure any how." When you know why you are doing what you are doing then you can stay motivated to continue moving forward.

Wright

Any final words for our readers?

Satchell

To your readers, I say, "Get motivated! Keep moving! Be a success!

Wright

I know our readers will try to stay as motivated as they can and you have certainly given them many good ways to do so.

Today we have been talking with Donna Satchell. She is a professional speaker, trainer, author and president of STARR Consulting & Training. STARR is an acronym for the product and service line, which is: Speeches, Training, Assessments, Resources, and Results. Donna believes that, "True success comes from reaching beyond one's grasp. It comes from reaching for the stars."

Donna, thank you so much for being with us today on *The Power of Motivation*! I appreciate the time you spent giving us your great insights.

Satchell

David, the pleasure was all mine. I thank you for selecting me to be a part of this project.

About The Author

Donna Satchell

Donna Satchell is a professional speaker, trainer, author, and president of STARR Consulting and Training. STARR is an acronym for her service and product line, which is: Speeches, Training, Assessments, Resources, and Results. Her programs and presentations are based on her insights into success which she developed during 20+ years working in corporate America. During that time she achieved many remarkable accomplishments while working at Clairol Inc. and Bristol Myers. Her successes include: 1) being the first administrative assistant to be promoted into a managerial marketing position at Clairol; 2) receiving several individual and team awards and; 3) being recognized as one of the company's experts on field-based promotional analysis and category management.

In May 2002 Donna left Clairol to pursue her desire to help others become more successful in their personal and professional lives. She provides training in customer service, team-building, public speaking and a variety of other business topics. She presents motivational speeches which inspire audiences to live more rewarding, fulfilling and successful lives.

Donna is one of the co-authors of a series entitled *Insights From The Experts*. It includes the following three books on leadership, time management and stress management: *303 Solutions to Dropping Stress and Finding Balance, 303 Solutions to Accomplishing More in Less Time and 303 Solutions to Developing The Leader in You.*

Donna is a member of the National Speakers Association, American Society for Training & Development and Les Brown Speakers Network. She is on the Advisory Committee for DeKalb Technical College.

Please visit www.STARRct.com for information about products and services as well as to view several videos of Donna's speeches.

Donna Satchell
STARR Consulting & Training
Phone: 770.498.0400
Email: info@STARRct.com
www.STARRct.com

Chapter 5

Excellence In Change Management

R. Bruce Bickel, Drs.

Let's be realistic. Our world is changing. It's not the same as it once was. My stepson and a couple of buddies were visiting us recently and I said, "You know, I hope you realize that your children will not have the same experience you did, growing up in our family. The world has changed."

My stepson and his friends replied, "What do you mean? Isn't this the way it's going to be forever?" So, we began to talk about the world situation, the many changes occurring all around us and about how one manages in the midst of change.

In a business context, there are several types of change that can arise. And there are two aspects of change management in which excellence needs to be cultivated. First of all, excellence needs to be applied to managing ourselves. We don't manage change—we manage ourselves. A changing business environment dictates that we learn to manage ourselves in the midst of a situation that we can't control. Secondly, excellence in a shifting environment demands that we learn how to merge ourselves with other people—how to work as a team.

Change

Let's start by considering the various types of change present in the business world. There is the knowledge change. You have a new product that you're offering your clientele. You simply tell them, "We offered you A but now we're going to offer you B." This is the easiest kind of change.

An attitudinal change is a bit more difficult. An example of a corporate attitudinal change might be a shift from service orientation to product orientation. Because attitudinal change can be emotionally charged, either positively or negatively, it can be more time-consuming.

Then there is a behavioral change. For example, a manager may encounter behavioral change when a particular employee is required to switch from working alone to working in a team setting. This is a change that is even more challenging.

Lastly, there is group or organizational change. It is the most strenuous and time-consuming of all. So, as we progress from knowledge changes to attitudinal changes to behavioral changes to organizational changes, we devote an increasing amount of time to helping ourselves and others cope with the change.

MANAGING YOURSELF - Change and Negative Emotions

You've heard a lot of people say, "Embrace change!" or, "The only constant thing about change is change itself." Well that's true; but let's be honest, change is much more difficult than these nice, pithy little statements suggest.

Here's my definition of change: **C**onstant **H**arassment **A**nd **N**egatively **G**enerated **E**motions. That's really what change brings about. So the real issue is, how do we manage ourselves in order to maintain excellence in the midst of change? After all, we've got to manage ourselves before we can merge ourselves with others to become an effective team.

There are four negative emotions that change can spawn. The first is fear. In the midst of change, fear is generated as we lose control of our environment. In reality, we don't have the foresight to anticipate every possibility, and we don't have the power to handle every situation. So, we play the 'what if' game and become fearful.

Secondly, there's anxiety. It's the fear that something we need will not be provided. "You mean, we're going to change and we're not going to do it the way we used to? What if I don't get the computers, or the support staff I need? How do you expect me to excel?"

Then there's resentment. We feel threatened by the lack of control we have over the situation. So, we look to place blame on someone else. "You know it's their fault—it's them. They're to blame."

Lastly, change can even stimulate mild depression. Change can feel so overwhelming that an individual panics and becomes hyper-introspective. Depression is a preoccupation with one's own situation, drastically reducing one's capacity to care about others, or to think clearly about the situation. "I'm not going to be able to make this work. I might as well give up now." These are the destructive emotions—fear, anxiety, resentment and depression—that can surface because of external change beyond our control.

Character and Negative Emotions

We return to our original dilemma: how can we maintain personal excellence amidst change in the workplace? As much as we focus on the external demands of a changing circumstance, the fact of the matter is, we can never manage change. What we *can* do is manage ourselves, and that is a function of character.

Let me show you what I mean. A change occurs. You feel a certain way then you act a certain way and after acting that way long enough you develop a thought pattern that becomes a habit. This is what happens when you take your initial cue from your emotions. For example, you're told to make cold calls. You feel insecure about this because you've experienced failure and rejection with cold calls in the past. You don't want to make these cold calls. The fear of rejection feeds your insecurity, and eventually convinces you that you are unable to make cold calls. Your negative feelings lead you to the habit of inactivity.

It's not that feelings are inappropriate. Feelings are neutral. It's what you do with them that counts. You can feel insecure and still fulfill your job description. You can feel insecure and be responsible to those counting on you. You can feel insecure and be excellent in the performance of your duties. How? By changing the way you think, not by following your emotions. That's why I say that managing yourself is really a function of character. It starts with disciplining your thoughts. If you think right, you'll act right. If you act right, you'll feel right. That's how you manage yourself in the midst of change.

Now, I suggest that you enter into a character covenant with yourself. A character covenant is an arrangement one makes with oneself—it acts like a plumb line. Those in construction know that a plumb line sets the standard from which all other measurements are taken. Set the plumb line for excellence in the midst of change. Say to yourself, "This is the way I'm going to think in the midst of change, because this is the way I want to act in the midst of change, because this is the way I want to feel in the midst of change." Manage your emotions by managing your thoughts.

Eight Principles and Eight Character Traits - Be a Follower

Allow me to outline eight principles of managing yourself in the midst of a changing environment. Each principle has a related character trait. As you exercise a given character quality, you'll be fulfilling the principle responsibility.

The first principle is: learn to be a follower. To be a follower, one must employ self-control. Being a follower means bringing your thoughts, words, actions, and attitudes into constant obedience to the benefit others. Being a follower means being mission minded.

I'm a graduate of the Naval Academy. In January of my senior year I took a course on leadership. Our professor began by dividing the twenty-five of us into five groups. Each group was to choose one outstanding historical leader to study during the next sixteen weeks. After thorough research, each group was to write a 300-page report about what made this person a significant leader.

Among our five groups, we chose Mahatma Gandhi, Jesus Christ, John F. Kennedy, Adolph Hitler, and Martin Luther King. Surprisingly, in the end, we discovered that the same three characteristics emerged from each leader. There was one particular characteristic, however, possessed by each of them that intrigued me the most. It was not their personality or their charisma that gave them their base of power, it was who or what they represented. To be great leaders, they became great followers. Take the example of Mahatma Gandhi. According to the research, he was a very quiet, unassuming man who didn't like crowds or making speeches. But Ghandi was self-controlled; he unwaveringly followed a mission outside of himself and much bigger than himself—the independence movement of India.

We need to be mission-minded too, using self-control and submitting to who or what we represent.

Be a Finisher

Next, be a finisher. Here is where you learn the character quality of responsibility—knowing and doing what is expected of you. Notice the word "responsibility" is made up of two words: "response" and "ability." A person who is responsible is response-able. Conversely, an irresponsible person is one who doesn't finish what she or he was given to do. Practically speaking, then, being responsible means that you don't start something you can't finish; and once you've started something you make sure to finish it.

After I got out of the Navy, having served in Vietnam, I went to work for The Fellowship of Christian Athletes. I was looking forward to working with the youth of America, and was excited when they assigned me to the city of Chicago. Within a fifty-mile radius, there were 325 high schools and twenty-seven four-year colleges. It appeared to me as a rich, fertile land, ready for the taking. So, I came up with an expansive and masterful plan of how I was going to win the city of Chicago. Quite honestly folks, it looked like a military assault.

One of my board members said, "Bruce, why don't you take this down to the principal at the local high school?"

So I did. The principal was a gracious, elderly woman. She looked at my elaborate plan, took off her glasses and said, "Son, I only have one comment for you."

I replied, " Pulitzer Prize?"

And she said, "No. Succeed in a few and fail in none."

She was trying to teach me to be a finisher. That was one of the greatest pieces of advice I ever learned. Inherent in what I had planned to do were things I couldn't finish. If you and I are going to be excellent in the midst of a changing environment we need to be responsible and finish what we've started.

Be Focused

Besides being a follower and a finisher, I also think it's important that we be focused. The character quality of dependability can help us be focused. Being dependable means doing what is expected of you, even if it means unexpected sacrifice,

Often people ask me how many missions I flew in Vietnam. My answer is that I flew one too many. On my last one I didn't make it back—my aircraft was hit and I crashed. I didn't know it at the time, but I crashed about 200 yards away from 3000 North Vietnamese troops. Because of the dense jungle between us it would take them two hours to reach me; but they never did. I was picked up in an hour and fifty-nine minutes. This is what happened: Once I crashed, I activated my emergency-landing transmitter. I was paralyzed by my injuries; all I could do was wait and see who would get to me first, not knowing if the rescue choppers were picking up my signal. But as I heard the enemy troops approaching, I also heard a Jolly Green Giant Air Force helicopter above. A paramedic dropped through the trees. He took care of my injuries and gave me shots of Demerol, while the enemy approached and began shooting at our position. This young man did more to me in one minute than any other human being has ever had done in my life. We both got into the basket. As we ascended through the treetops, the enemy over-ran our position and started shooting up at us. Though the aircraft took six or seven hits, none of us were injured.

Just before I passed out from blood-loss and shock, I looked into the eyes of my rescuer—a young man who I later learned was a Native American, a high school drop out from South Dakota. I said, "Why did you come down and get me, if you knew the enemy was so close?"

This is what he said," Sir, because I said I would."

That's dependability. Let me tell you, I'm very grateful I served in the armed forces of a country whose people fulfill what they say they're going to do, even if it means unexpected sacrifice. We need this kind of excellence in our own character, so the people over us and under us know they can depend on us.

Become Your Own Reward System

Here the emphasis is on the character quality of thoroughness. Realize that each one of your tasks will be reviewed; but don't work toward an external reward. Set your own standard of excellence and find your reward in the internal satisfaction of knowing that you've attained it. When you work for an external reward, you work in spurts.

I have salesmen who report to me and the one thing I've told them is not to work for the bonus. The bonus is the *result* of your work, not the *reason* for your work. If the bonus is your goal, when the year ends you just have to start all over again. By contrast, you need to exercise patience, endurance and thoroughness so at the end of the day you can say you finished what you were given to do. At the end of the week, at the end of the month, at the end of the quarter, and at the end of the year you can say you finished what you were given to do. You can feel the inner satisfaction from a job well done. In the midst of change you're going to see external upheaval and inconsistency all around you. If you look to externals for your reward, you're never going to be motivated toward excellence. Become your own reward; be thorough.

Become Your Word

The fifth principle I'd like us to consider, is being true to your word. The character quality associated with this principle is that of trust. Trust affords others confidence in you and your word. It secures an assured reliance on your integrity and honesty. Let me take you back to my jungle experience. While lying there, something kept going through my mind. As a Naval Aviator, I was always told that if I got shot down they'd come and get me. I must have said to myself a million and a half times, "I know they will come. I'm going to hang on for one more minute because I know they will come. I know they will come because they said they would." And you know the end of the story—they came. You see, that's assured reliance on someone else's word. In the midst of change people need to be able to bank on something solid and unchanging. They need to be able to lean on the trustworthiness of your word.

Build Double Loyalty

Furthermore, it's essential for us to learn how to build double loyalty. The character trait here is obvious. Loyalty, however, is not something that can be fostered when things are going well. Loyalty is developed during hard times. When you express your commitment to others, despite difficulties, then you are exemplifying loyalty.

Now, what do I mean by "double loyalty"? Let me give you an illustration, because double loyalty is paramount in leaders and managers. Let's say I need two more staff members. I go to my boss, make my presentation, plead my case and he says, "Sorry, we're in a cost containment mode. You can't hire any more people for the next two years." I return to the twenty-five people in my department who are eagerly waiting to see if I won. My response to them is, "They did it again. They don't understand us. They won't give us what we need." In this situation, I have built single loyalty—loyalty to our departmental mission alone.

My role as a leader, however, is to build loyalty not only to our mission but also to our corporation's mission. What I should have said was, " We've been given a more demanding assignment to fulfill, but with the same number of people we have right now. How can we do it?" With these words, I'm building loyalty into my departmental mission and into the mission of the company. That takes self-control. And if you're going to manage yourself and be excellent in the midst of change, one of the things you've got to learn is to build double loyalty. And remember, it happens during difficult times.

It makes me think of a time when I played football in the Navy. I played with Roger Staubach, who was in the class ahead of me. Roger was a great quarterback and had won the Heismen Trophy the previous year. He was anticipating winning it again this year—his senior year. We were playing in our first game against Penn State in a rainstorm. We were ahead seven to six, when Roger went down with two minutes left in the second quarter and a torn Achilles tendon. I'll never forget the look on my coach's face when he gazed down the bench at me. At the time I was number two quarterback and probably had no more than six minutes of varsity experience under my belt.

All the coach said to me was, "No pressure on you, but the season is yours. Just don't fumble."

We beat Penn State and went on to win a couple of more games. It was hard to fill Roger's shoes. Then one day, while visiting Roger in the hospital, I learned an important lesson. Beside his bed he had two pairs of shoes of differing size. He had me try on the bigger pair and asked me if I could run in them. No—they were too big. He had me try on the smaller pair. They felt great; they were my size.

After a moment of silence I looked questioningly at Roger and asked, "What's the shoe bit about?"

He said, "Bruce, don't try to fill my shoes. You're a good athlete and I want to help you become better and start helping you build on the things you're good at."

So, Roger began teaching me how to improve my mental game and how to maximize my strengths. I learned a lot at Roger's bedside. I learned about double loyalty. Roger demonstrated loyalty not only to me but also to the team. By helping me achieve personal excellence, he was helping the team achieve excellence. When you find yourself in the midst of corporate change, build double loyalty.

Manage Your Fears

Another principle that we touched on earlier is managing your fears. Courage is the character quality that comes into play here. I learned in Vietnam that courage is not the absence of fear, but it's the ability to fulfill one's responsibilities despite one's fears. In other words, you can still do your job even though you're afraid.

An African hunter told me, that when a pride of lions goes out in the early morning to hunt, they take full advantage of the fear they can evoke in their prey. The oldest male lion, with his big mane and ominous appearance, parks himself in full view. The rest of the lions hide behind bushes, some distance away and wait. When a herd of antelopes arrive on the scene, the big lion lets out his roar. As it echoes through the valley, the antelope freeze momentarily, not knowing that the old cat doesn't have any teeth! But his roar is enough to instill fear and send them running into the jaws of the younger, waiting lions.

What are your fears? And how do you manage your fears? If you don't know what your fears are, you won't be able to manage them. And if you don't manage your fears, you fears will devour you. Know your fears—face them head on with courage.

Choose the Harder Right Rather Than the Easier Wrong

Lastly, if we're going to maintain excellence in the midst of change, we need to be able to choose the harder right rather than the easier wrong. To do this we need boldness, which fortifies us to do what is right for ultimate victory, in spite of present opposition. In essence, it's doing what's right just because it's the right thing to do. Now, when you exercise the character quality of boldness, you will be modeling leadership that is very unique and deeply needed in our culture. I have this principle locked into my management style. I give no consideration to profit or loss, when confronted with issues involving ethics, duty, or right and wrong; and I confess that choosing the harder right does indeed demand boldness.

Conclusion

The best way to manage yourself as a leader in a changing environment is through character. Are you starting to feel like I'm painting a picture of a super-hero? Well, I am. That's the exciting thing about living a life built on good character qualities and noble principles rather the whimsy of emotion. We are, in fact, capable of bigger and better things. When you and I exercise self-control, responsibility, dependability, thoroughness, trust, loyalty, courage and boldness, we place a plumb line in our lives that keeps us steady and strong when circumstances around us are turbulent.

When you display these traits, you will be a leader who cares more than others—this is wise. You will be a leader who risks more than others think is safe; you will be a leader who dreams more than others think is practical, and you'll be a leader who expects more than others think is possible.

It's your choice. If a leader chooses character, then change will not change him or her. Change will only become a forum in which excellence is manifested. If our country is ever to regain its leadership role in the world, it's going to need organizations of character and those organizations must be lead by people of character.

MERGING WITH OTHERS - A Definition of Teamwork

Now that we know how to manage ourselves in the midst of change, how do we merge ourselves with others, building a team that can weather change? The word "teamwork" comes from the Greek word *sunergos*, which is made up of two words: *sun*, meaning "together" and *ergon*, meaning "work." Our English word, "synergy" is derived from this Greek word. So, "teamwork" can be defined as engaging in a coordinate action toward a common goal. Teamwork is imperative for the complete success of a group mission.

Let me explain how this works with a story from my childhood. I grew up in the hills of West Virginia. Pittsburgh for me was the big city. To go to Pittsburgh I put my shoes on and came out of the hills. One of the main attractions for me was the county fair. I loved horses and there were horses at the county fair. I remember one particular year when there was a magnificent Clydesdale in the horse-pulling contest. When they hooked up all the iron and put the buckets of coal on the sled, this horse pulled 4500 pounds, winning the gold medal. The second horse pulled 4000 pounds. Now, the crowd was really charged up to see what the two horses could pull together. According to betting theory, you'd add 4000 to 4500 to get a total of 8500. I wanted to see that pair pull 8500 pounds. But they didn't—they pulled 12,000 pounds! That's teamwork. It means that the total in a combined effort is greater than the sum of the individual parts. With teamwork, one plus one equals three. Everyone working together can accomplish more than each as an individual can accomplish.

Action with an Attitude

Though the word "teamwork" is identified in the dictionary as a noun, we know from the horse-pulling example that it involves lots of different actions. But in the realm of change management, building a successful team means more than busy-ness; it means being propelled by right thinking. I want to examine four attitudes that will merge individuals into a team of excellence, fit to handle change.

Don't Think of Yourself More Highly than You Ought

A successful team player doesn't think more highly of himself than he ought to think. He thinks of himself with sober judgment, realistically accessing his own strengths, and readily affirming the strengths of others. He sees how he fits within the context of the group, and how his portion of work contributes to the completion of the group's ultimate goal.

In 1975 I had the tremendous honor of debriefing Navy POWs returning from Hanoi, with the intention of helping them reintegrate into American society after five or six years of grueling imprisonment. I have their permission to share with you some of the things we discussed.

After spending several days with these 331 POWs I was astounded by the fact that I never heard one of them talk about personal survival. Their unified attitude was, "We're all going to get out of here or none of us will." Now that's synergy. Even at the threat of torture, loyalty to the group was their number one goal. Even when facing six to fifteen months in solitary confinement, remaining strong to preserve the cohesion of the group was primary.

One guy summarized his motivation as, "whatever it took to help the man next door." In this extreme setting, fear of letting down one of the other guys was a powerful motivator; so was guilt. Though we typically think of fear and guilt as unhealthy motivators, that's not always the case. When one of the guys did break, they again turned their attention to what was best for the group. The man was reassured by the others that he'd do better next time. The man disciplined his thoughts to not harbor self-pity. Positive guilt was applied to help him muster the fortitude to face future torture. "Because these guys need me," was what it boiled down to time and time again. What a powerful example of not thinking of yourself more highly than you ought-of soberly accepting your place within the group. Do the trials you meet now seem a little less daunting? Do the changes ahead of you now seem a little more manageable?

Availability

Availability is the willingness to assume a responsibility in order to benefit other people. If I'm really committed to a common mission I need to be available to people. Somebody might have a need and say, "Bruce, I just can't do this, will you help me?" In this situation, I need to be available. You see, availability is the management of interruptions—it costs—you have to be willing to put something aside for the sake of somebody else.

In my present capacity as a grant maker, I award grants to foundations and charities. At one time, I was sitting around with a group of grant makers, talking about our job description. As we went around the table, each person gave a nice fifteen-minute harangue until they got to me. They asked, "Bruce what do you think your job description is as a grant maker?"

I said, "I think my job description is to be available. "

They replied, "If you do that people will call you on the phone and make an appointment. They'll bug you!"

I asked, "Isn't that what we're supposed to do? Aren't we supposed to give the money away? That means I need to be available to find out who needs the money."

For me there is something bigger at stake here than interruptions. The group mission surmounts my personal comfort and timetable. That's how availability contributes to the synergy of teamwork.

Diligence

Diligence is the third essential characteristic to being a successful team player. To me, diligence is visualizing each task as a special engagement and pouring all my energies into its accomplishment. After I graduated from the Naval Academy and before I went to flight school, I had the privilege of being the freshman football coach for six months. They said I could choose a couple of varsity players to assist me. Some were sure I'd pick the outstanding linebacker who had been our most valuable player. But I chose another guy—I chose Bill. Bill had only just started his senior year. He played defensive end and he had a peculiar habit of using a considerable volume of tape. He taped his ankle, his knees, his wrist, his elbows and fingers. He even wore a neck brace. He looked like a mummy on the football field. But Bill was one of the most diligent guys I ever met. One practice, before a game while the rest of us were throwing the ball and running routes, I spotted Bill off by himself. He took a piece of chalk, drew a square, and stepped inside it. That was his warm-up! So, I went over and asked him what on earth he was doing. He explained, "I'm visualizing tomorrow's game." What? He continued, "My job is to not let anyone get around me so that Gene can make the tackle. I'm visualizing my task and I want to be diligent about it." That's why I picked Bill. I wanted my players to learn the character quality of diligence.

In the corporate setting, diligence works the same way. What I do I must do well and bring it to completion because one of my team members is depending on that in order to complete his/her job. The degree to which I'm successful will affect the degree to which the group succeeds. Interestingly, when Gene was given the MVP award, he gave special recognition to Bill saying, "If Bill hadn't done his job, I wouldn't have been able to do mine."

Dependability

The fourth attitude I want to touch on in the context of team building is dependability. I know I addressed this earlier in the realm of managing oneself but let me give you a collective example here. I once asked a classmate of mine, who was a Navy Seal, "What is it that makes a Navy Seal so unique? What is it that makes you so dependable?"

He answered, "We have this thought pattern that says, 'Complete to complete.' In other words, individually we complete our own assignments but collectively we complete our group assignment." The degree to which they completed their personal tasks was the degree to which the group would fulfill their common mission. That's integrated dependability.

Loyalty

Lastly, let's turn our attention to loyalty—the final attribute necessary in making a team. Allow me to further elaborate on the Navy Seal motto. While the phrase "complete to complete" encapsulates dependability, it also refers to a rigorous form of loyalty. If one Navy Seal goes down another is able and ready to step in and finish the job. Because the completion of the mission demands it, each person is required to train fully in his own area and in the areas covered by his mates—they cross-train. They purposely groom their skills so that in a moment of crisis they are free to exercise stalwart loyalty. Now that's how to get a job done!

Conclusion

The best way to merge yourself with others in a changing environment is by donning these attitudes of excellence: loyalty, dependability, diligence, availability and not thinking of yourself more highly than you ought. Stellar teamwork is action initiated by reformed attitudes. When this kind of teamwork becomes your corporate tradition, there's no limit to your success. Friends, the ability of the human will to bend one's mind to right thinking is a source of empowerment that is grossly underestimated and underutilized—not just in personal achievement but in collective achievement as well. Change doesn't have to be our nemesis. It can be the backdrop on which shines the spotlight of character excellence.

Now this is the law of the jungle—as old and as true as the sky;
And the wolf that shall keep it may prosper, but the wolf that shall
break it must die.
As the keeper that girdles the tree trunk, the law runneth forward and
back—
For the strength of the pack is the wolf, but the strength of the wolf is
the pack.

—Rudyard Kipling

R. Bruce Bickel, Drs.

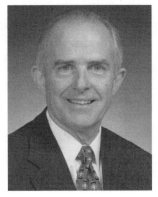

Dr. Bruce Bickel is president and founder of Transformational Leadership Group, LLC, and Senior Vice President and Managing Director of Private Foundation Management Services, PNC Advisors, Pittsburgh, PA. Bruce graduated from the United States Naval Academy in 1966 with a B.S. in Electrical Engineering. After serving in Southeast Asia in an aviation capacity, he served as Vice President of the Fellowship of Christian Athletes. Bruce addresses issues concerning character and ethics as related to organizational effectiveness.

Dr. R. Bruce Bickel
President
Transformational Leadership Group
P.O. Box 24567
Pittsburgh, PA 15220
Phone: 412.389.1315

Chapter 6

Wally "Famous" Amos

THE INTERVIEW

David E. Wright (Wright)

Wally Amos was born in Tallahassee, Florida, and lived there with his father and mother until he was twelve. He then went to live with his Aunt Della, who first baked chocolate chip cookies for him in her Manhattan apartment. As a senior at Food Trades Vocational High School, Wally dropped out to join the U.S. Air Force.

While in the Air Force he earned his G.E.D. high school equivalence diploma. That certificate helped change his life, the G.E.D. diploma made him eligible to train at a New York secretarial school after he was honorably discharged from the service.

Wally Amos is an icon and his name is a household word. As founder of Famous Amos Cookies in 1975, and the father of the gourmet chocolate chip cookie industry, he has used his fame to support educational causes.

Since 1979, Wally has been national spokesman for Literacy Volunteers of America he is also a board member of the National Center for family literacy and communities and schools. His latest enterprise, Uncle Wally's, has been critically acclaimed by the media and consumers alike for tasty, high quality muffins. Wally, thank you for being with us today on *The Power of Motivation.*

Wally Famous Amos (Amos)
Well David it's my pleasure, thank you for wanting to talk with me.

Wright
Wally, you seem to have always been around success and achievement. I understand you worked as a theatrical agent at the William Morris Agency, where you worked with Simon and Garfuncle and the Supremes. What did you learn working with superstars?

Amos
Well, when I was working with them they weren't necessarily superstars. I was the first agent to work with Simon and Garfuncle and I was with the Supremes on the very first day before they even had hit a record. I later worked with Marvin Gay so I worked with a lot of artists early on and watched them develop. I had been around show business since 1961 when I started working with the William Morris Agency. So, I have seen some big ones, I've seen some not so big ones, I've seen all kinds.

One of the things I have learned is people are people and it doesn't matter what your title is or how famous you are we all have the same issues we are dealing with. I have learned to treat people with respect—the way I want to be treated—because in reality *everybody's* a superstar.

Wright
Was there anything about the ones who have been really successful that you could see in the very beginning or—

Amos
Well, when I first heard Simon and Garfuncle I knew those guys were going to be a major, major act. First of all their look—they had a very unique look. Arty Garfuncle was this tall guy with hair going every which way and Paul Simon this little guy who looked like Napoleon. The blend of their music was just absolutely out of this world. That combination said to me, wow! these guys are really hot and they are really going to go somewhere.

Now, regarding the Supremes, I had been working with Motown and I wanted an artist who had a hit record on Motown called Brenda Holloway. Brenda had a record called "Every Little Bit Hurts" and we wanted her for a tour. I called Ester Edwards, Barry Gordy's sister

[Barry Gordy started Motown Records in 1957]. Ester was handling the management of Motown acts at the time and I offered her five hundred dollars for Brenda Holloway for a seven-day workweek. We supplied bus transportation; they had to pay their own hotel.

So, Ester, who had been trying to sell me these three little girls she had, called the Supremes, said, "We will give you Brenda if you'll buy the Supremes."

I said, "But Ester, the Supremes do not have a hit record and I can't have them if they don't have a hit record, they are not going to be any value to me."

So we talked on and on and she said, "We just recorded them, let me send you a test pressing." I agreed.

There was no Fed-Ex overnight back then and she sent it special delivery. We got it a couple of days later, and listened to it. During those years everything Motown produced was a hit record and so when we heard it we thought it was "in the grooves" as they say. We decided to go for it. I offered her eleven hundred dollars for the two acts—six hundred for the Supremes to be split three ways and five hundred dollars for Brenda Holloway. The Supremes' record came out on that tour. I can remember seeing them in at the Atlantic City Steel Pier toward the end of the tour. They were just crying saying, "We are never going to have a record, we are never going to have a hit, everyone's got a hit but we are never going to have a hit." Well, their first record "Where Did Our Love Go" came out on that tour, then they had six number one records and never looked back. Diana Ross was clearly the leader of the group; she had a certain charisma, a certain entertainment attitude about her that said she was a superstar. It was wonderful; it was a great experience. The Supremes were one of the last acts to have a hit record for Motown.

Wright

Knowledge, someone has said, is power, and you are a teacher and host of fifty episodes of state-of-the-art programs for adult basic learners on PBS stations nationally. Do you think knowledge is a major step towards people's ability to achieve and follow a success path?

Amos

I think so. I would also question whether knowledge is power. An automobile is not transportation—it is only transportation when you drive it.

Wright

That's true.

Amos

Knowledge is only power when you use it—when you use it properly. But to have access to knowledge, to understand the importance of knowledge, and to be willing to do whatever it takes to avail yourself of that knowledge, I think is absolutely critical.

During the time I have done work with literacy and helping adults learn how to read and creating awareness for literacy I have never said I was, "fighting illiteracy"; rather, I'm always, "promoting literacy." I always look for a way to give it the positive spin because I think what you resist persists and if you constantly focus on the negative then that's what you are going to have in your life. I think that education is the foundation of a well-lived life—of a meaningful life—no question about it. I'm really proud of the work I have done with literacy. Since 1979 I've been the national spokesperson for literacy, and I've been a literacy advocate since 1979.

Wright

I had read that since '79 you had been the spokesman for literacy volunteers.

Amos

Well now here's the thing, there were two major organizations that worked with adult non-readers: one was Literacy Volunteers of America and the other one was Laubach Literacy International. Those two organizations merged in 2002. These organizations are now known as ProLiteracy Worldwide, headquartered in Syracuse. Both organizations were headquartered in Syracuse previously so their headquarters remained in Syracuse but now it is just one organization.

Wright

Can you tell us a little bit about their work, especially the volunteer part of it?

Amos

Well, what they do is it is one-on-one tutoring for adults as well as youngsters. I have known of high-school teenagers and college students who have actually tutored adults also. So, if a person knows how to read and has the desire to teach someone who cannot read to read then ProLiteracy Worldwide has the skills, the tools, and the resolve to train that person in the techniques of teaching an adult how to read. Adults already have a vocabulary—you're not dealing with a blank page—they've got experiences, they have context, and ideas so the progress an adult makes is much quicker because they are also motivated. When adults finally decide and have finally made that step to come forward and be taught, that decision was one they had thought about for a long time. Once they recognized they finally had to make that decision they acquired a thirst for knowledge and a real strong desire to learn.

There are techniques to learn about how to teach. It requires a lot of patience and a lot of love and respect for adults who have spent all of their life perhaps never really acquiring literacy skills resulting in low self-esteem.

David, I have spoken with so many tutors who are volunteers who have described new students who come in with hunched shoulders and head down, showing all the signs of low self-esteem and the negativity attached to that. The tutors have said, "Man, watching that person and sitting across from them or next to them learn how to read is like watching a flower bloom because the more they learn, the more they grasp the alphabet and the English language, and the more they are able to master those words on pages, the more their posture becomes erect and their attitude changes." They see a transformation right before their eyes. It's a wonderful experience for the volunteers—both people get something from it. Lasting friendships are formed also, not only with the student or the tutor but also with their respective families, so the ripple effect goes on. When that person learns how to read it changes their life—it changes their relationships with everyone in their life. There's a wonderful quote that says, "Volunteering is reaching your hand out into the darkness to pull another's hand back into the light only to discover that it's your own."

Wright

Well, I'm glad to hear that because I just signed up to be a volunteer in Sevierville, Tennessee.

Amos

Oh you did? You pulled me right into that.

Wright

So now I can't wait.

Amos

You are going to love it. They are just the most wonderful people and so are you for doing that. There is another quote that says, "Give a man a fish and he eats for a day; teach a man how to fish and he eats for a life time." I have often thought when you teach an adult how to read you are literally giving them the tools and the skills to enhance their life for the rest of their life. It's wonderful.

Wright

Wally when you speak to corporations, associations, and universities you talk about such things as inspiration, motivation, and overcoming adversity. What caught my attention was one of your topics titled "Spirituality in Business." Do corporations really care about spirituality?

Amos

Well, some of them do and some of them don't. It's taboo in some areas, but it's more and more accepted now. I remember one day a number of years ago I was taking a morning walk in Phoenix, Arizona—it was a Sunday morning—I am passing churches and the parking lots were just overflowing. It occurred to me that many of those people worked in corporations; some of them were even CEOs, vice presidents, treasurers, and human resource people. Every Sunday they go to church and then, when the workweek starts, they don't want to acknowledge God in their business—only on Sundays. These same people who run corporations have a spirituality that they try to deny.

I'm finding now that more and more people are dealing with their spirituality. They are now understanding that life is more than just the material—it's more than what we can see, touch, feel, smell, or hear—there's something behind all of that. There's something that's responsible for the breath in your lungs every day, something that formulates the words and pushes them out of your mouth, and there is absolutely something to all of this that causes your heart to beat twenty-four hours a day.

More and more corporations and more and more CEO's are acknowledging their spirituality. That's a great signal for everyone else in the organization to acknowledge his or hers also. There was a time when I heard people tell me not to talk about God. I wondered why not—God is all there is; but now I never hear that anymore. My talks are always laced with spirituality and I get more and more people after my talks who come up and thank me for acknowledging the power greater than all of us—the power of the one who created us.

I think we are becoming more and more open to spirituality in the workplace and there are companies now that do entire seminars on that.

Wright

Great. You have an audiocassette tape out titled "You Have the Power." In the program you talk about unlocking your dreams and experiencing success, embracing love, and letting go of fear. What really caught my attention though were your comments about not getting bogged down with expectations. What do you mean by that?

Amos

Well, you have to have *some* expectations, I suppose; but so often we expect things to be a certain way. When those expectations don't turn out the way we anticipated it absolutely throws us for a loop—we cannot function and we get just totally out of whack.

I always believe you have to do your best, and then you have to let go and turn it over to God. We may have a plan but God may have another plan. I'm just so happy when God's plan overrides my plan. It has happened so many times—when I have wanted it to go a certain way but it didn't. The way it turned out was so much better. As a matter of fact I created a quote for myself years ago saying, "Life is never really what it seems—it's always more." It's always more—God knows what you need before you do and he has promised that He will provide it and provide it in abundance. We don't always know what's best for us.

You can have expectations but I think you can't necessarily be married to your expectations because there's might be something far greater than what you expect. You have to be open and receptive to that—you have to allow a little serendipity to come into your life, those unexpected gifts.

Wright

My minister used to tell me people would tell him, "God doesn't answer my prayers." He used to tell them God answers all prayers, but sometimes He just says, "No," or, "Wait."

Amos

Absolutely, absolutely. And you know, sometimes He answers prayers in different ways; He doesn't always answer them when you want Him to answer them. As a matter of fact, this morning and every morning, I read a book titled *Streams in the Desert®* by L. B. Cowman. It's a wonderful book on faith and this morning, the chapter I was reading was about patience. We have this idea that we are suppose to be doing something all of the time—we are suppose to be making things happen. You can't *make* anything happen; you can prevent it from happening sometimes but you can't *make* it happen. Often, what we do is interfere with it happening, so it's okay to be still, it's okay to be patient. Just wait and see what God has in store for you.

Wright

Well, you certainly have the reputation of someone who walks the walk.

Amos

Sometimes I trip up and sometimes I get impatient. Patience is one thing I am challenged by because I want it and I want it *now*, I need it now because I've got all of these other pressures, so I forget sometimes

Wright

One of the greatest statesmen in our time I think is Colin Powell. May I read a quote of his?

Amos

Please.

Wright

Talking about you, he said, "Drawing on his own life experience over a quarter of a century of passion for enriching his fellow man Wally gently hammers home the point that the stones we occasionally find in our paths are really building blocks not stumbling blocks." Those words must have made you awfully proud.

Amos

It did, what a neat guy he is. When he gave me that quote he said, "Wally, you know everybody calls me for quotes and he said I just don't usually do it but I'm going to do one for you." That quote was for my book *The Cookie Never Crumbles*, so I was very honored and very pleased.

Wright

I was going to ask you about *The Cookie Never Crumbles*. Could you tell us a little bit about it? I know it's a bestseller.

Amos

It has helped some people along the way. The book was published in 2001, and is a series of personal antidotes structured in the form of recipes. There is the entrée and I'll talk about an experience I've had that corresponds to the dish. After that I'll give the recipe on how I overcame the challenge involved in that particular episode of my life. Those answers on how I came through are really structured, for example: A half teaspoon of commitment, a cup of desire, positive attitude, those kinds of things. It's a neat little book and it's easy to read. Just little short antidotes so you can really turn anywhere in the book and get a meaningful message I think.

Wright

That's great. You know, almost every person I talk with about success and achievement points to some form of goal setting as the first step to success. Do you agree with that?

Amos

I think we set goals because we need a method. For example, if you want to go to Cleveland how are you going to get to Cleveland unless you make a plan for how you're going to get there? I think people establish goals in different ways. We don't necessarily always have a very clear cut way of how were going to get somewhere. Everybody's just different in relation to their goals and how they achieve them. But, I think, either subconsciously or consciously, you are always establishing goals.

Now I don't necessarily mean you sit down and say, "At three o'clock March first I'm going to accomplish this and I'm going to do that." I had a goal a long time ago to get back in the cookie business. That was really a goal I had and I got back in it too. I started this company under a new name that ended up not being cookies but muffins and it turned into Uncle Wally's but I still wanted to be in the cookie business. I held to the though—to the idea—that I really wanted to sell cookies again because I'm really passionate about cookies and about chocolate chip cookies in particular. So, I'm back in the cookie business. But, it took a long time to have that come about—a lot of set backs, a lot of ups and downs—but I just held to the desire. Along the way I met people who bought in to that dream of mine to that goal of mine and people who were very instrumental in helping me who had the skills and what not to help me accomplish my goals. It's like a discussion about whether you make a decision or don't make a decision. It's a decision. Not making a decision is making a decision because you decided not too decide.

I think goals are the same way you could have a goal and you could just be sitting down thinking, "Wow! You know, I want a new house." That thought is a seed of a goal and then it kind of germinates and grows. You water it and then you start figuring out how to do it and other people come into your life to help because the only thing you can do by yourself is fail.

Wright

Well, your Aunt Della is probably glad—she's probably smiling down from above and saying, "He's back in the cookie business."

Amos

Oh yes, yes. She has always smiled down. I've always thought Aunt Della was my guardian angel who saw me through the rough spots. I'm convinced that this time around she's going to be more than a guardian angel because this venture is named after her, so she has to have a very active part in having this come to be.

Wright

The only reason I asked the question is, of course, I believe in goal setting. I'm sixty-three now and some of the things that have happened in my life that were successful happened because I was open to them and didn't resist when the opportunities came. I didn't plan for them but sometimes opportunities just jump up in your face. I think we all have a decision to make whether we are going to follow our instincts or just resist them.

Amos

That's serendipity in life—you just never know where it's going to come or how it's going to come. I'm telling you, though, if you have faith, if you trust, if your intentions are good, and if you are doing everything you can to succeed at your goals and realize your dreams it will happen eventually; but you've got to be patient and you've got to know it's not going to come on your time it's going to come on God's time.

Wright

Wally with all your success and achievement, did you ever think that someday you would actually become famous?

Amos

It never crossed my mind; that was never a goal.

Wright

Isn't that something!

Amos

It was never even an idea to become famous and yet I became very famous.

Wright

I see your picture on things and when I recognize your picture I say, "Hey, there's Wally!"

Amos

I always tell people if I can succeed on the level that I have, then surely everything is possible, I mean without a doubt *everything* is possible.

Wright

With the things you are doing I can just imagine why people talk about you the way they do and about the things you do. Do you have any plans for the future you can share with our readers and listeners?

Amos

My plans are to continue to be a part of the Uncle Wally's team and develop Uncle Wally's muffin company into a successful company. My plans are to really establish Aunt Della's to be a major, major cookie company. My plans are to be a good father, and to be a good husband.

I don't have any long-range plans, things just kind of come along. I grab some and watch some go by. I guess if I have a long range-plan it is to get all of these businesses really in a good solid state so they're supporting my family and me financially and I don't have to travel quite so much. I'm on the road seventy, eighty, sometimes ninety percent of the time. I would just like to stay home a little bit more and just enjoy Hawaii and enjoy my wife.

Wright

The last time I talked to you it was cold in Tennessee and you were sitting on your back porch watching the ocean.

Amos

Well I'm in Houston today, David, and it's a little chilly here. I'm watching the freeway today.

Wright

I remember that conversation very well. I was freezing to death and you were looking at the ocean.

I really appreciate you being with us today. It's always a pleasure talking to you.

Amos

Anyone interested in more information about Wally Amos can go to my website www.wallyamos.com. There is a lot of detailed information there about Aunt Della's cookies and Uncle Wally's muffins including my lecture schedule and, my books and whatnot.

Wright

I try to keep up the best I can with readings I'm suppose to be doing daily and you have got some great tapes. One is called "Faith" and the message is about beauty and the wonder that faith can bring into a person's daily life. I think they are taken from the *Daily Word Magazine* aren't they?

Amos

Yes, the faith messages are *Daily Word* messages and the "Let Go Let God" tape also has *Daily Word* messages.

Wright

I was also reading about those; I intend to get them.

Amos

The "Let Go Let God" tape, David, is one of the most powerful things I have ever done. I mean truly, truly, truly, my friend.

Wright

There's the one on "The Man With No Name." Did Dr. Deepak Chopra write that?

Amos

No, that's my book. I wrote that when I was going through a lawsuit. I think Deepak might have given me a quote for it.

Wright

So it was written during of your trials and tribulations going through the lawsuit.

Amos

Going through the lawsuit when Famous Amos sued me.

Wright

Well, I'll get those tapes too then. Now, I may look funny in the Wally melon top hat.

Amos

But who cares? My daughter thinks I look funny in mine but I don't care. What you think of me is none of my business it's what I think of me that matters.

Wright

I really do appreciate it; it's always a pleasure.

Amos

It's my pleasure. Thank you.

About The Author

Wally "Famous" Amos

Originally, Wally Amos, a true cookie lover, baked his cookies to share with his friends. Once he perfected the ultimate chocolate chip cookie, he started using them as his business calling card and as thank-you gifts. As Wally made his rounds in the entertainment business, more and more of his friends and clients asked for another bag of cookies. Finally, Wally launched the Famous Amos® Cookie Company in 1975.

Wally "Famous" Amos
www.famous-amos.com

Chapter 7

Unleash the Animal in You
Success Lessons from
Clifford the Yellow Lab

Terry Nicholson

Since the idea for this book came from my Labrador retriever, Clifford, we'll start our journey through the animal kingdom with a look at what my four-legged best friend has taught me over the years. I learn more every day from Clifford.

Clifford Enthusiasm—It's Not Just for Breakfast

Our journey to make you "Wildly Successful" starts with Clifford at his usual post. He's eleven years old and a certified member of the family. In fact, we used to throw birthday parties for him.

Let's start by focusing on Clifford's love for his job. Clifford likes to sleep next to my side of the bed. He's there every morning, and I believe that's because he's so dedicated to his work. It's his way of showing me he's always ready to go and ensuring that he'll be on time for work.

Clifford's job starts as soon as the alarm sounds. Sometimes he's so eager that he wakes me up before the alarm—now *that's* ambition. Can you imagine waking your boss in the morning because you can't wait to get to work?

Once the alarm signals the start of the day, Clifford thrusts his chest onto the side of the bed to make sure I'm getting up. He will even place his wet dog nose under my arm and hurl it upward with all his might. This technique usually elicits a groan from me as I slap the alarm clock out of commission. In the meantime, Clifford trots to the top of the stairs and impatiently runs in circles.

If I don't get out of bed, it won't be long before Clifford is bedside for round two. Before my eyes have closed again in post snooze-button bliss, Clifford is once again hurling his chest against the bed. If that doesn't work, I know I will be hit in the face by a big, wet dog tongue. Nothing says good morning like a sloppy one from your dog! That's all the motivation I need to get going.

As soon as my feet hit the floor, Clifford's back circling the top of the stairs. He'll look downstairs, back at me, back downstairs, and then back at me. I can almost hear him saying, "Let's go! I have work to do!"

Once I make my way to the stairs, it's "go time" and Clifford flies down in what seems like warp speed. As he hits the hardwood floor at the bottom of the staircase, he goes into a hyper-slide in which he appears to lose all control of his legs. After Clifford regains his footing, he runs back to the stairs to check my progress and then cruises to the front door. It's amazing how much energy that non-coffee drinking dog has from the first moment of the day. He goes from zero to sixty before I can roll out of bed. By the time I open the front door, he has his eyes on "the prize."

Clifford leaps off the front porch and bolts across the yard toward the newspaper. He circles his victim and leans down to make the scoop. It's a challenge today because it's Sunday, and he must contend with the extra weight. He clenches that huge Sunday paper in his jaws and lifts his head. After a few short trial steps, Clifford tears off toward the house with his jaws gripping the paper. He bounds up the stairs and drops the prize at my feet, radiating pride for another job well done. Sometimes he seems to be smiling.

Why Don't You Run in Circles at the Top of the Stairs?

Are you that enthusiastic about waking up for your job in the morning? Do you go to the top of the stairs and "run in circles"?

What I learned from Clifford was an important lesson I applied to myself—love what you do. What if we all got as excited as Clifford every morning? Wouldn't the world be a thrilling place?

If you're not this excited about your job, why not? Is it the job or something inside you? Either way, the answer is the same—change. If your job is bringing you down, causing too much stress, or ruining your happiness, change it. Happiness is priceless. Don't waste your time doing something that doesn't leave you fulfilled and wanting more.

Is that challenge somewhere inside you? Does your attitude cause you to get buried under mountains instead of moving them? Then, find your enthusiasm and be like Clifford. He is uncontrollably excited about the opportunity to do the same mundane task every morning.

What are your unique opportunities every morning? These are the things that should launch you out of bed and jumpstart your day. Clifford was the only dog with the opportunity to retrieve our paper that morning, and the pride this opportunity generated in him was palpable.

You are the only one with the opportunity to serve your clients' needs every day. Why not take pride in this idea and make your service memorable? What are the motivators to provide excellent customer service that will fling you out of bed each morning?

This idea goes beyond business. What can you learn each day? How can you grow? Those are the thoughts that should get you enthusiastically out of bed.

Be Happy to Be Alive

Clifford's story is a perfect place to start our journey together as we discover the secrets of success hidden within Mother Nature's inspiring world. Why? Because it's about the kind of enthusiasm I hope you'll have when you finish this book—the kind of enthusiasm that radiates the, "I'm just happy to be alive today" feeling we get from lovable dogs like Clifford. Each day truly *is* a gift, so we need to be enthusiastic about our opportunities and radiate excitement at every turn.

This idea can be intimidating. If Clifford can wake up with unrestrained enthusiasm for the opportunity to trudge out into the yard and carry back that heavy and difficult-to-hold Sunday paper, I certainly should be able to get excited about the opportunities I'm presented with each day.

When I have a particularly grueling day ahead, I think of it as my "Sunday paper." I may not be looking forward to a particular sales call or assignment, but it's a challenge I can conquer if I approach it with a dose of Clifford enthusiasm. It makes the morning much brighter when you can wake up with that kind of enthusiasm. If you don't wake up with it, then create it within yourself. Take a few moments before you go to bed to make a short list of things you were thankful for during the day. Make a list of what you are looking forward to the next day. Then put this list where you'll see it in the morning. By thinking about the things that went *right* in your day, you'll go to sleep thinking about the good stuff rather than what may have gone wrong. You'll wake up feeling more enthusiastic about the day ahead; and then the list of things you're looking forward to will help you get off on the right foot. Wake up each morning, read your list, and be thankful for your opportunities. Starting your day with this type of enthusiasm will help you conquer your "Sunday paper."

Think of the impact a big dose of "Clifford enthusiasm" will have on everyone around you. We all love working with pleasant, positive, and motivated people, and that's what you'll be. Positive attitudes are more infectious than the flu, so if you carry that enthusiasm with you throughout the day, chances are someone else will be infected. Everyone around you will accomplish more, and you'll end your day with an immense feeling of satisfaction and pride—just like Clifford when he triumphantly drops the Sunday paper at my feet.

Don't be afraid to take pride in your accomplishments. I'm not suggesting you run out to boast about yourself to anyone who will listen. While Clifford certainly doesn't walk around the house gloating over his feat with the Sunday paper, something in his behavior tells me that when he drops the paper on the floor, he knows he has done a good job. He doesn't have to wait for me to pat him on the head. So, be your own cheerleader—pat yourself on the back. If you don't take pride in what you do, you can't expect anyone else to, either.

Think about all of the people in this world who overcome extreme challenges and emerge with fantastic attitudes and an even stronger sense of self. There are people dealing with hardships I can't imagine overcoming, and yet they have the strength to surmount it all and succeed. They're all around us.

Lance's Journey Back to Life—And Across France

One of my favorite examples of this is American cyclist Lance Armstrong, whose story is one of perseverance and ambition. In 1996, Armstrong was diagnosed with an aggressive form of testicular cancer. When the cancer was found it had already spread to his lungs and brain. The future looked bleak for his survival, let alone a return to competitive cycling.

Yet after two surgeries and extensive chemotherapy, Armstrong lived to return to cycling. He trained continuously, not allowing his ailment to hold him back from winning the ultimate in cycling—the tortuous, 2,400-mile Tour de France. Three years after treating his cancer and fighting back to health, Lance won the Tour de France in 1999, and then repeated his feat in 2000, 2001, 2002, 2003, and 2004!

It's truly an amazing story, but Lance is only human. If he can overcome so much, why can't you? While most of us won't face challenges that severe, we also won't ever achieve as much. Why is that?

Dogged Clifford Determination

When you start each day with Clifford enthusiasm, you'll begin accomplishing more and appreciating each day more. Eventually, though, you may encounter unexpected challenges, or you may find that something is harder to achieve than expected. It's inevitable—nothing is ever as easy as it seems. At times like these, you can excel by discovering the second trait I learned from my trusty friend: Clifford Determination.

We wimp out all the time—admit it—when was the last time you quit something because it was "too hard" or you just didn't understand it? We all do it. Think of all the New Year's resolutions you never kept and all the times you said, "I'll get around to it." Everyone will slink away from an occasional challenge when things get difficult—I've been there.

Nobody runs out looking for difficult tasks; but maybe you should. How else are you going to grow unless you continually face new challenges? Some believe that to truly grow as a person, you should do something difficult every day. When I get into these situations, I step back and take a moment to consider how Clifford would approach things.

I'm not saying I consult my dog on difficult business decisions. Yet I do occasionally think about how he would handle a tough spot. The answer is always the same: with determination.

One of Clifford's favorite pastimes is digging. While he loves it, my yard does not. At any given time, I can almost guarantee Clifford will have left his mark somewhere in the backyard. I like to think he's digging for buried treasure, and, boy, would I be a proud owner if he finds one! Yet the truth is I'm never sure what he's after. What can you and I take away from this bizarre habit that will help us through our struggles to succeed?

What strikes me about his digging is Clifford's determination. Once he sets his mind to digging, he won't stop until he finds what he is after, be it a rock or a bone he had buried. I've even seen him dig in the rain as his hole fills with water and collapses on him. Nothing deters him.

That's inspiring. Sure, Clifford's only a dog who may not know any better, but I prefer to think he knows exactly what he's doing. He sets his heart, or his nose, on a goal and doesn't quit.

I think about that determination when I'm facing a difficult challenge. Would Clifford give up or keep digging? If my dog can do it, why can't I? So I keep digging. My challenges don't seem as bad when I throw a little "Clifford determination" at them.

Try it next time you're in a bind or stuck trying to overcome a challenge. Think about that "determined Labrador" inside you who just wants to keep digging and pushing. That's the kind of determination you need to succeed.

The number of success stories from people who refused to give up is astounding. Colonel Sanders was rejected 1,009 times by investors before he found someone to back him and his chicken dreams. Can you imagine a world without KFC®? Walt Disney was rejected 302 times in his quest to find someone to fund Disney World®. Imagine if Disney had given up after his 301ˢᵗ rejection. Twenty-three publishers rejected Dr. Seuss's first children's book. The lucky twenty-fourth publisher sold millions of copies.

If you keep trying, you'll eventually get a "yes." Each obstacle or challenge simply reduces the amount of "no's" you have to go through to reach that "yes." Every setback propels you one step closer to achieving your goals.

Everything that happens to you, good or bad, carries a message. If you've done something right, learn from it and discover how to do it right again and again. If you've done something wrong or fallen upon a great challenge, learn from it so that you can avoid it in the future.

If you're after a certain job, don't give up until you get that job offer. If you're pursuing a big account, don't quit until it's yours. *Persistence* is your strongest ally in getting what you want—don't stop until you've found what you're after—keep digging!

Clifford Loyalty

Loyalty—it's another characteristic dogs are known for, and Clifford has it. He's there to wake me up in the morning. When I walk through the door at night, he's there to greet me. I know I can count on Clifford—I know that when I sit down, he'll be there to sit beside me. I know I can trust Clifford—he's never going to do anything to harm or betray me. His dependability is reassuring.

Can people count on you?

Adopting these ideas of loyalty and dependability will attract others to you. A good maxim is, "To find success, help others find success." If you are loyal to others and help them succeed, you will succeed. When you are loyal to others, they will be loyal to you.

People who go through life striving to get ahead by stepping on the backs of others don't get far. Those who do usually don't stay at the top for long. Why—because no one is loyal to them. They succeed at the expense of instead of at the gain of others, so nobody is in their corner.

Think of what you can do to help others succeed. It could be as simple as teaching someone in your office to use the copier or volunteering to tutor someone in your spare time. Anything you can do to help others succeed will ultimately help you succeed. I've seen it happen many times.

While your road to success won't be easy, it will be considerably smoother if you have others to help you along the way. As with Clifford, it's reassuring to have someone loyal to depend on. Be loyal to your family, friends, and coworkers, and they will be loyal to you.

Yet loyalty comes with a price. To truly be loyal to someone, you may have to do things they won't like. You may have to tell them when they aren't behaving properly or that the choice they are thinking about making isn't the best one. When you're loyal, you're responsible for looking out for the well-being of the other person. When you keep an eye out for others, they'll keep an eye out for you. Loyalty means being faithful to someone or to something.

Another important part of success is being loyal to yourself. Do you let others push you into things you would not normally do? Do you get pulled into situations where you feel forced to go against your typical behavior? In these instances, you may not be remaining loyal to yourself.

Think about peer pressure. Alcohol, drugs, and reckless behavior can be the partners of peer pressure. If you're in a situation where there is pressure to take part in something you don't want to do, simply take a cue from Clifford. It's difficult to get him to do anything he doesn't want to do. If Clifford doesn't feel like walking, he's not going to walk. If he feels like running, he's going to run. The idea is to stay loyal to yourself. Don't let others pull you in directions you wouldn't normally go.

You're in charge of your path to success—don't lose sight of your goals—don't let damaging behavior send you off course.

Clifford Lessons

Here are successful behaviors you can discover from Clifford to make you Wildly Successful:

- Remember how important your attitude is. If you approach each day with a positive attitude, you'll be able to achieve more and you'll enjoy each day more than the last.
- Don't be afraid to face the challenges that come before you. Instead of slinking away, attack them with vigor. Just think of "Clifford vs. the Sunday Paper."
- Take pride in what you do. Be your own cheerleader—let yourself know you've done a great job. There's nothing wrong with patting yourself on the back without gloating.
- Be enthusiastic about your opportunities. Each new day is loaded with potential new experiences, knowledge, and opportunities.
- Don't give up! Stay determined—keep digging for what you are truly after in life.
- Stay loyal to those around you. Help others and they will help you.

Terry Nicholson

Motivation and inspiration flow through Terry's veins as an award-winning speaker, trainer, columnist, and author. After honing his sales skills for 6 years with Results; Tom Hopkins, Terry became the 1st National Sales Trainer of the 1st publicly held HVAC company, where during his tenure sales grew from $67 million to $688 million. He then became VP of Sales for Clockwork Home Services, Inc., where he sold $18 million of consulting services in only 12 months. As a member of Clockwork Home Services' Board of Directors, he helped build 10 businesses that have become the fastest growing of their kind in only 5 years with over $130 million in annual revenue. Today, he is also President of Success Group International, a division of Clockwork Home Services, and author of the highly acclaimed *Unleash the Animal in You.*

Terry Nicholson
Success Group International
7777 Bonhomme Ave, Suite 1800
St. Louis, MO 63105
Phone: 314.862.8181
www.unleashtheanimal.com

Chapter 8

The Power of the Dream

Conway Stone

THE INTERVIEW

David E. Wright (Wright)

Conway is a professional speaker, author and dreamer based in Louisville, Kentucky. With a bachelor of arts degree in psychology, a bachelor of arts degree in religion, and a master's degree in human development and potential, Conway has spent the last thirty years studying personal growth. He works with organizations and individuals who want to accomplish outrageous dreams. His books, *Follow Your Dreams* and *Dream High*, have been translated into twelve languages and more than 100,000 copies have been sold.

Conway, welcome to *The Power of Motivation*.

Conway Stone (Stone)

Thank you very much David, I'm excited about being here.

Wright

So, I'll ask you a really important question that's appropriate to begin a book about motivation: What is your definition of motivation?

Stone

David, motivation is anything that moves you. Motivation could be getting up in the morning for some people—they're excited about the day and ready to move on; they're motivated already and that's fine. Other people are motivated by the fact that they've got little children running around the house and they want their children well clothed, well fed, and able to go to school; so they get up and go to work. Others are motivated by money or fame or success.

The problem is, many of us are motivated from outside sources. For example, the job says, "You've got to go," and, "You've got to be there by eight o'clock." The boss says, "I want this done by two o'clock," and most of us react to these motivations that come from outside of us. When we signed on to do a job or work with a particular organization, we have agreed to these outside motivations, but they come from outside ourselves nonetheless.

If we can set aside outside pressures and become motivated from inside ourselves then the entire dynamic changes. We want to complete this job by two o'clock (as given in the example earlier) because it will be done right and on time. If you can make that motivation come from within it will make your life much, much easier. That's why I'm excited about being a part of this book, and about the power of motivation.

Let me just throw in one other thing David. This is one of the best quotes I use when talking about motivation. I believe there was a saying in ancient Greece that went, "When Apollo stood up and spoke, people would stand up to applaud; but when Paul stood up to speak people would stand up to march." That's the group I want to be a part of—a group of people who are ready to stand up and march!

Wright

So what is the biggest single thing we can do to motivate ourselves?

Stone

The biggest single thing we can do to motivate ourselves is to get a powerful dream. Most people have dreams but they're vague notions in the back of their head. Their dreams are nothing more than wishes such as, "I hope it's going to happen." Their life—their problem—are bigger than anything else. They say things such as, "I've got to get to work, so I can get this bill paid," or "I've got this illness in my life," or

"My Aunt Suzy is dying." These problems are bigger than anything else in their life and they work on those problems.

The best thing we can do is to create a dream inside of us that is so big it compels us forward into the future—a dream so big it's bigger than any other problem we currently face; now our motivation is not coming from outside but it's coming from within.

Wright

So why are dreams important?

Stone

Dreams are important because a dream takes these vague notions out of the back of your head and gets them down on paper. When you put that dream on paper, now you've got a picture of where it is you want your life to go. Rather than trying to create a life based on outside pressures of family and work and houses, and problems, we have an internal motivation—a dream inside of us—that is bigger than all of those problems. And if you have a picture of that, you know where it is you want to go.

Dreams are also important because they're about the future—they compel us into the future. They get us doing things that will create a better tomorrow.

Dreams are also important in that they get everyone on the same page. When you have a dream written down and you have a picture of your dream, then your spouse and you both know where you're going; then your boss and you both know where you're going; and your employees and you know where you're going. Dreams compel everyone in the same direction.

Wright

Are there steps to making our dreams come true?

Stone

I've outlined a number of steps in my book, *Follow Your Dreams*. The book has been translated into a number of different languages and has sold around the world. As always I'm excited about sharing this vision, especially with your readers here.

The first step to turn dreams into reality is you've got to have a *vision* of what it is you want to do. The ancient Jewish writing says, "Where there is no vision, the people perish..." (Proverbs 29:18). Of course the opposite of that is also true: "with a vision, people can flourish." A vision is nothing more than a picture of what your dream will look like when it's finished—let's get a picture of your dream.

The second step to turning dreams into reality is you've got to be *willing to bet your life on your dream*. Life is made up of nothing more than time and energy. If you are willing to exchange your time and energy for your dream then it can come true. If you're *not* willing to exchange your time and energy for your dream then don't follow that dream, because it's not going to happen. Your dreams must be more important than watching television on Saturday night or going out to eat with your friends. Your dreams must be more important than the other things you're doing. If you're going to follow your dream, you've got to be willing to exchange your life, your time, and your energy for that dream.

One of the best examples of that is, of course, Martin Luther King Jr., who was willing to devote his entire life, and the life of his family for that matter, to make his dreams come true.

The third step for turning dreams into reality is you've got to be willing to *focus your life*. I was flipping through a magazine once and it had a big picture that said, "Focus or die." This is true in business and it's also true in following our dreams.

Let's put it this way: How many horses can you ride at one time? Unless you belong to the Chinese circus the answer is that you can only ride one horse at a time. If you try to ride sixteen you end up getting thrown off, trampled and killed. The same is true with dreams, if you try to do sixteen or eighteen things at once, you end up dead— immobilized—you can't move. But if you can focus on one dream and bring all of your power, your energy, your life, your family, and your resources to bear on one direction, you can accomplish it.

People ask me questions like, "I have a dream of a house and a car and being able to travel. How do I focus on all of that?" Well, my reply is for them to write a mission statement. Write a one-sentence statement of why God has placed you here on earth.

My mission statement says, "I am here to create a positive difference in the world in which I live." Under that mission statement I have a number of dreams: I have a dream for my family, I have a dream for my travel, I have a dream for my business, I have a dream for my writing, I have a dream for my money, I have a dream for my real estate and I have some dreams for helping other people. I have several dreams, but every one of them is designed to "create a difference in the world in which I live." That way I've got everything focused and moving in the same direction. "Focus or die" is an adage for business, but it's also an adage you and I need in following our dreams.

The fourth step for turning your dreams into reality is you've got to be willing to *write them down*. Most people have vague notions in the back of their heads; I call them a "wish list." People think of dreaming as nothing more than, "Oh, I'd like to do this someday." But I'm telling you, if you take that vague notion and write it down, it becomes extremely powerful.

Most people say they want to be rich. Well if you write down the words, "I want to be rich," on a piece of paper, it begs the question, "What does 'rich' mean?" Rich may mean, "I want a million dollars." Rich may mean, "I want to work thirty hours a week and have the rest of the time off so I can play and enjoy life." Rich may mean obtaining a certain cash flow. But you cannot reach the dream of being rich without first defining what you want.

Once you define what "rich" is such as "having a million dollars," then that begs the question, *when* do you want this million dollars? If you answer, "Well, I want to have a million dollars by the time I'm sixty years of age," then that begs the question, "how old are you now?" Do you see that simply writing down the dream can start you in the process of trying to figure out where you are now, where you want to be, and how much time you've got to get there.

And now the question comes, how are you going to get a million dollars? What are the steps I need to take to make this happen? Writing the dream down creates that process—writing your dream down is very important.

The fifth step for turning dreams into reality is having a *strategy*. You've got to have a specific one- two- three-step strategy for moving from where you are to where you want to be.

So, you have a dream of becoming a millionaire, now it's time to develop a strategy to achieve this dream. You might need to increase your income, decrease your spending, and make better choices with your investments. You might need to get a second job, buy a piece of real estate or do something else that can make this dream come true. When we're talking about strategy we're always talking, about *time,* we're always talking about *focus*, we're always talking about *money*, we're always talking about *people*, we're always talking about *government regulations*, and we're always talking about *managing time and energy*. These are some of the elements that must to go into your strategy.

The sixth step for turning dreams into reality is you've got to *expect to win*. So many people go through life expecting to lose. They've been hit and they've been hurt so many times that they *expect* to be knocked down. They don't expect their dreams to come true.

I was watching basketball one time—the University of Kentucky was playing—and this guy had the ball. He was going to drive toward the basket, but there was a defender between him and the basket. This guy started toward the basket but he knew that the defender was going to foul him; he knew that the defender was going to try to block him. As he drove to the basket he didn't even shoot the ball; he was expecting to be hit. Too many of us follow our dreams but we're expecting to be knocked down. We're not expecting to win—we're expecting to fail. That mindset has got to change if we're going to turn those dreams into reality.

The seventh step is *persistence*. Persistence towards your dream is one thing that will make it come true. Most of us know the old adage from Calvin Coolidge that persistence is everything. Persistence will help you move toward your dreams when everything else fails. Before we move on, here is the quote for you:

"Nothing in the world can take the place of Persistence. Talent will not; nothing is more common than unsuccessful men with talent. Genius will not; unrewarded genius is almost a proverb. Education will not; the world is full of educated derelicts. Persistence and determination alone are omnipotent. The slogan 'Press On' has solved and always will solve the problems of the human race."

Calvin Coolidge—U.S President

Many people think persistence is just hanging on. Well, you can't just "hang on" to the way things are right now because the way things are right now are both good and bad. You'll be hanging on to the good things you've done and the bad things you've done as well. If you just "hang on" you're going to hang on to the reality the way it is currently—problems as well as their solutions.

When I think of persistence, I think of setting up a strategy of specific steps toward making dreams come true. I think of creating a feedback system that will tell you where you're facing problems. Then you can create a system that will take you around those problems toward your dream. That's what I mean by "persistence."

Those of us who are married have in-laws—a built in feedback system (funny but true). We have people in our life who are a feedback system and who want to point out where our problems are. When you're following your dreams, especially in business or personal development or professional development, these systems are very important.

When you start creating a system to move toward your dreams and a system to get around the problems you're facing, you're moving past persistence and into what I call *perseverance*. Those people who persevere make their dreams come true.

The eighth step for turning dreams into reality is you've got to have *faith*. Faith is simply believing in something you cannot see. Faith is the bookend to the first step—vision. Vision is having a picture of where you want to go; faith believes you're going to get there. The way I like to describe faith is in the following story: A captain leaves New York harbor sailing a big ship to Hong Kong. When he leaves New York he cannot see the port of Hong Kong for ninety-nine and nine-tenths percent of the journey. It's not until the last quarter of a mile that he can ever see the Hong Kong port. But he has faith that if he does the right things and goes in the right direction he will get to the port of Hong Kong. That is what faith is; and that's what you and I have to have if we're going to follow our dreams.

Wright

So what is the most powerful thing we can do to make dreams come true?

Stone

Well, I'm glad you asked, David. A lot of people see these steps and they understand the points I'm making here but what I've found to be the most powerful is the simple word—*affirmation*. Affirmation is a one-sentence statement of your dream—what you want to come true.

Stating that sentence in the positive, stating it in the present as if it's already happened, stating it in the right now, can really propel your dreams forward.

Let me explain what I mean. If weight loss is the goal, a lot of people end up saying, "Well, I'd like to lose thirty pounds." That's a negative statement. No one wants to lose anything. No one wants to be forced to do something. So what I ask people to do is turn that sentence around. If you weigh 190 pounds, instead of saying, "I want to lose thirty pounds," begin with stating what you *want* to weigh. Say, "I weigh 160 pounds." That one-sentence statement is very positive and very powerful.

Psychologists tell us that physically, emotionally, spiritually, and mentally, we start moving to the most dominant thought that we have in our mind. By stating what your dream looks like when it's finished, stating it in the positive, and stating it in the right now, it becomes your predominant thought. If you say your dream in the positive sense, you're creating a new dream, a new vision, and a new picture in your mind. Then you'll start moving toward that dream.

Let me just say a couple more things about affirmation. Psychologists tell us we all have pictures in our head of how things are. We know how clumsy we are, we know how much we weigh, and we know what social status we live in. If you create a new picture in your mind through affirmation, then you can create a new place where you're going to live—"I'm going to live at 160 pounds instead of 190," or, "I'm going to live in a new house instead of this house." By stating your dream in the affirmative you can create new pictures in your mind and you will physically, emotionally, and spiritually move toward those pictures.

There are three ways I recommend for people to write down their affirmation statements in order to create a new reality. The first way is to write the "I am" statement such as—"I am 160 pounds." The second statement to write is the "I see" statement—"I see myself slim and trim at 160 pounds in a firm healthy body." The third way is to write the "I feel" sentence—"I feel my best weighing 160 pounds in a firm healthy body." If you write the "I am," the "I see," and the "I feel" statements you'll start changing the pictures you have in your mind and you'll start changing the attitude you carry around with you. You'll start changing the dream you have for your life. Affirmation statements are very, very, motivational.

Wright

I can see how this is motivational. I see a lot of bad stuff happening in our world. What is their motivation?

Stone

Well, it's obvious that there's a lot of bad stuff happening in the Middle East—there's a lot of terrorism happening around the world. There's a lot of drug selling, and killings on our streets in the major cities in our country. There are similar people in your organization, in your company, maybe even in your family. Understanding their motivation can help you deal with them. Find out what their belief system is—investigate the premise they start out with.

Let me just explain it this way: My mother always buys whole milk. When I ask her why, she always tells me:

1. Milk is a good source of calcium,
2. Two percent milk is all just water, so it's no good,
3. Milk is good for your digestive system.

Now, if you believe those three things as she does, then buying whole milk is just the natural outcome of that belief system. It's a correct action; her logic is very, very, good.

Well, I believe that two percent milk is the best milk to buy. You ask me why, I will tell you:

1. I was taught in college that American men don't need a lot of milk because it has a lot of fat—a lot of cholesterol—and therefore it's not good for the heart.
2. I was also taught that you cannot drink enough milk to get all the calcium you need; you need to take a vitamin.

Based on my belief system I always buy two percent milk.

You can see that nothing's wrong with our thinking—nothing's wrong with our logic—but our actions are different. The difference is our belief system—the premises we start with that create different actions.

So when I talk to people about motivation, I always ask them what their starting point is. What is the belief system you're starting out with? Your logic can be very good, your actions can be very logical, but your belief system may be wrong. So, people who're selling drugs to kids have a belief system that tells them selling drugs is the quickest and easiest way to make money. They believe if someone else gets hurt it's their own fault, not the fault of the drug dealer. Well, their belief system is set up to allow them to act in ways that are very destructive. People in the Middle East believe that bombing other people to make a point is okay. That belief system has caused them to commit terrorist acts and nothing is going to change until they change their belief system. The point is this: if the belief system is wrong, the actions will be wrong.

Wright

You've given us a lot to think about, regarding dreams, can you tell us a little about *your* dreams. What motivates you and what are some of your future dreams?

Stone

I appreciate that. From the time I was a very young man, I've always had a lot of dreams. When I left high school and went to college, I dreamed of three things: Living in a foreign country; Getting a degree in psychology, and I dreamed of marrying a good southern girl. When I graduated from college five years later, I had two college degrees, a bachelor of arts degree in religion, and a bachelor's degree in psychology. I had lived for a year in Nigeria, Africa, which allowed me to study a culture completely different from my own. Marrying a good southern girl wouldn't come for several more years, but two of my three dreams had come true.

In understanding that process I've had some very sharp psychologists from around the world teach me to write down dreams in one place, so I developed a "dream book" I've had for the last twenty years. A dream book is simply a book where I write down every dream I want to accomplish—especially those I want to accomplish within the next twelve months. I've written down dreams of cars and houses and land; I have dreams of a net worth, of traveling, of the books I'm going to write, and of completing a master's thesis. I have dreams of touching a number of people through my speaking and through my writing. I have all these dreams written down in one place. I also have a picture of each one of those dreams in my book. I have affirmations; "I am," "I see," "I feel," and I also have strategies for accomplishing each dream; all of this is written in one dream book.

I can tell you that I'm dreaming of traveling to Belize to speak this year. I'm dreaming of writing two more books and I'm dreaming of going to Montreal Canada in January and speaking to three thousand people. I'm dreaming of buying about thirty acres of land that's connected to a National Forest, and one of these days I'm going to retire to that place and teach at a local Christian College. Those are some dreams I have and I've written them all down.

While we're on this subject, at my website, www.dreamhigh.com, there is a place to download pages for a dream book. On one page there is a place for a picture of a dream. The other page has a place to write the dream down in one sentence, a place to write a one- two-three-point plan of action for accomplishing that dream, and a place to write the three affirmation statements, for each dream. I call the pages a *Dream Action Workbook*. A workbook can be purchased from the web site; but it's not necessary to do that—the pages can be downloaded at no charge. Anyone can create his or her own dream book; dream books are very, very powerful.

Wright

Conway, I know some people will never get around to buying a book and downloading the pages, do you have a *Dream Action Workbook* people can buy so they can get started with their dreams today?

Stone

Yes, David, the *Dream Action Workbook* I sell has a place for you and your spouse to put your picture on the front; it comes with a mission statement page and an example of how to get started. It also has a place for you to write down twenty dreams. Then I've enclosed a compact disk (CD) that has an audio section where I list 230 dreams you might want to follow. The CD also has downloadable refill pages you can print out as you reach your dreams and need more pages to add more dreams. The refills are also downloadable in English, French and Spanish. Anyone can phone my office at 888-899-5353 or order from our website at www.dreamhigh.com.

Wright

So how can we motivate others? You talked about outside motivation and inside motivation and it seems to me that motivation that comes from outside isn't very good. As a business owner, however, I have to motivate people as an outsider; how can I motivate others from within?

Stone

As a business owner and as a team leader of any kind you've got to understand that people are going to do things for *their* reasons not for yours. That's a hard thing for us as business people to swallow, because we have this big dream, we want people to buy into our dream and help us accomplish it. Yet you have to understand that people will only work with you for *their* reasons. Most people know the adage that says, "Everyone is tuned into the radio station called WIIFM, which stands for 'What's in it for me?' " Once you understand that, then we can begin to have people work with you to accomplish your dream.

First we need to find out why people are there working for you. Some people are there because they want a paycheck on Friday. So you explain to them, "If you want a paycheck on Friday, then you have to show up on time, you have to do what you say you're going to do, and you have to complete this much work, so you can get a paycheck on Friday." Now you're using *their* motivation—their excitement about the paycheck—to motivate them.

Other people are motivated because they want to do a good job— they were raised to work hard and do well. They did well in school and they want to do well in your company—that's their motivation. If you, as a business owner, understand that, you can tap into their internal motivation. All you've got to do is explain to them what "doing well" means. Doing well at my company means: showing up on time; doing what they say they're going to do; accomplishing this much work; doing it with a positive attitude, and doing it in a consistent way.

Other people are motivated because of loyalty or because of teamwork. They want to be part of a team—they want to be a part of something bigger than themselves. The business owner can easily come in and paint a dream—paint a picture—of what this team is going to accomplish that no individual can accomplish alone. So, start painting with words, start painting with a picture of where you're wanting this team to go, what this business will look like a year from now, how each person is a part of that process and the dream cannot be accomplished unless each individual does his or her part. Now you're taking the internal motivation of loyalty and being part of a team and being a part of something bigger than themselves, and you're tapping into that as a leader. You're also helping to motivate people forward.

Wright

Well, since you're a motivational speaker and do many other things having to do with motivating people, can you give us a little motivation to close this conversation which, by the way, I have enjoyed tremendously?

Stone

I certainly do appreciate that, David, and I'm obviously honored to work with your people. I believe in the power of motivation and I believe in the power of individual dreams, so I want to encourage your people to dream big dreams.

Let me just say a couple of things here. In 1969 the United States of America put two famous Americans on the moon—Neil Armstrong and Buzz Aldrin; both touched the moon. The truth is, however, that NASA employed 33,929 anonymous Americans to put two famous Americans on the moon. People like you and I—the average sales person, the average business person, the average school teacher, the average taxi driver, the average nurse—who nobody knows, who're not going to be rich and famous—these are the ones who make this country what it is. We are the ones who create the jobs, we're the ones who make the hospitals, the schools, the churches and the communities work around this nation. We're the ones who pay the taxes. The everyday folks are the people who get the jobs done. The famous people may go around getting their picture in the paper; but rest assured it's the anonymous Americans who make things happen.

The only problem is that too many of us are walking around living lives of quiet desperation not accomplishing the dreams we have inside of us. I want to say to everyone who is reading this: *you are not here by accident!* *You are here by divine appointment!* Get excited about the dreams God has placed in your heart, whatever they are—paying off the Visa bill, taking your grandkids to Disney World®, traveling to Europe, starting a bed and breakfast, buying a new car, traveling the world, going fishing out west, going deep sea diving, taking a cruise, retiring early, creating a net worth of a million dollars or two million dollars or creating a program you can teach in the local colleges—whatever your dreams are, follow them with all you have, because dreams *can* come true.

Abraham Maslow, one of the early American psychologists says this: *"The story of the human race is the story of men and women selling themselves short."*

You are more than you think you are. There is so much more that you can accomplish, and I want to encourage you to follow the dreams you have inside.

Let me close with one poem I read recently. Nelson Mandela was in prison for twenty-seven years. When he came out of prison, he could have been bitter, he could have been angry, he could have come out fighting, but he came out of prison with this quote by M. Williamson:

"Our worst fear is not that we are inadequate, our deepest fear is that we are powerful beyond measure. It is our light, not our darkness that most frightens us. We ask ourselves, 'Who am I to be so brilliant, gorgeous, talented and fabulous?' Actually, who are we not to be? You are a child of God: your playing small doesn't serve the world. There is nothing enlightening about shrinking so that other people won't feel insecure around you. We were born to make manifest the glory of God within us. It is not just in some of us, it is in everyone..."

Wright

Today we've been talking to Conway Stone who is a professional speaker, dreamer and author. His books, *Follow Your Dreams* and *Dream High* have been translated into twelve languages and have already sold more than 100,000 copies. You can find out more about Conway by going to his web site, www.dreamhigh.com.

Conway, thank you so much for taking all this time with me this afternoon to talk about something that's very, very important to each of us individually, as well as our country, and our world *The Power of Motivation*.

About The Author

Conway Stone

Conway is a professional speaker who works with individuals and organizations who want to accomplish great dreams. In pursuit of his own dreams Conway has lived and taught in Nigeria Africa, Tokyo Japan and St. Petersburg Russia. He has started his own company, founded a nonprofit organization and authored two books, *Dream High* and *Follow Your Dreams*. His books have been published in 8 countries and sold over 100,000 copies. Conway has been called the "Ambassador of Enthusiasm."

Conway Stone
Phone: 1.888.899.5353
www.dreamhigh.com

Chapter 9

Only One Form Of Motivation Has A Lasting Effect! The Rest Is All Temporary.

Rick Houcek

THE INTERVIEW

David E. Wright (Wright)

Rick Houcek's singular company purpose is: *To provide high-octane, world-class strategic planning systems for business and life,* helping Top Gun leaders, teams and individuals to succeed, "on purpose, most of the time," rather than, "by accident, some of the time." He does this four primary ways: (1) facilitating his *Power Planning*™ strategic planning retreats for small and mid-size companies, (2) leading his *Passion Planning*™ workshops for ambitious individuals on self-motivation, personal life planning, and goal setting, (3) delivering high-energy motivational keynotes, and (4) one-on-one success coaching.

He has coached entrepreneurs, CEOs, presidents, and senior executives for more than ten years, and is former president of Ross Roy Advertising, an Atlanta ad agency and division of the $700 million

Ross Roy Group. A University of Missouri graduate, he is a member of the National Speakers Association and has been recognized in *Who's Who Among U.S. Executives* and *Who's Who in Georgia.*

Rick is married and passionately devoted to his soul mate, Robbie, adores his awesome grown twins, Val and Chip, and has four fanatical life passions: his family, his personal health and fitness, helping others prosper through his business and friendships, and playing competitive baseball on a traveling men's team.

Rick, welcome to *The Power of Motivation.*

Rick Houcek (Houcek)

Thank you, David, I'm honored to be here.

Wright

Let's get right to it. You've spoken on motivational themes for many years – you've studied it, you've witnessed it, and you've lived it. Tell us what you feel are the main *sources* of human motivation – that can provide the fuel a person needs to *achieve*?

Houcek

This is a great place to start – you hit my hot button right off the bat. This is simpler than most people think – but it's not the answer the masses want to hear. It's singular, really, not plural. There is only <u>one</u> source of motivation that fuels a person's achievement, not several sources. And it's the only kind of motivation that works reliably and has a prayer of extended life: it's the kind that is *self-generated...internally-produced* – motivation that comes from *within* you: <u>Self</u>-motivation. Why? Because it's the only motivation *you* control. All other forms of motivation are externally-induced, meaning they come from some outside, external stimuli that you do <u>not</u> control.

We mistakenly think we are motivated by external events and other people: that a near auto accident, for example, will make us buckle our seat belt in the future...that hearing about our dream job opportunity will cause us to pick up the phone, get off our butt and take action...that a rainy weather forecast for tomorrow will push us to cut the grass today...or that a tough-grading teacher will make us study harder for the big exam. All that is baloney, not one pinch of it is true.

If it were true, it would universally work for everyone. But it doesn't. Why not? Because every person makes individual choices to suit themselves. Many people involved in auto accidents or near accidents do buckle up afterward, some for the rest of their lives. Others for only a few weeks until the memory wears thin. Still others don't change their behavior one iota, continuing to not wear a seat belt as they always have done. So the event had no universal impact. It had different impacts on different people...that brings us back to *individual choice*. Each person – exposed to the same external event – made an individual choice as to their self-motivation regarding the wearing of seat belts.

The bottom line is: people, events and "things," all from the outside, don't motivate us. Leaders can't motivate followers...coaches can't motivate athletes...teachers can't motivate students...parents can't motivate their children...doctors can't motivate patients...events don't motivate anyone...and on and on and on. No person – regardless of position, power, wealth, or influence – can motivate another person – unless that other person *chooses* to be *self*-motivated. And that choice comes from *within*. Period, exclamation point.

Wright

Is there other proof of this? More examples that can illustrate your point?

Houcek

The proof is everywhere. The world is chock full of "average Joes" who were exposed to the same opportunities for success, the same smart and powerful people, the same killer ideas as the real winners were – but they did nothing with it. That's an individual, internal choice. Of course, few of them see it that way. Most will blame everything but themselves, but it's the truth. Losers seldom see reality – that they are their own worst enemy.

More proof: criminals seem to be unfazed by the threat of prison – they rob liquor stores anyway. People still tell lies, despite the embarrassment and pain of getting caught. Monsters like Adolf Hitler, Saddam Hussein, and Osama bin Laden still terrorize people and countries, risking violent backlash and possibly their own death. U.S. prisoners of war know full well that their captors will torture them to get critical information, but brave and loyal soldiers resist anyway. And what mother hasn't felt like she's talking to a wall when her kids ignore her stern orders and do what they darn well please, oblivious to the threatened penalty. So, yes, the proof is all around us.

A few years ago, I gave a speech on self-motivation to a small group in Boston and covered this particular point in detail. One audience member was getting noticeably restless and fidgety in his chair, and seemed to be bursting with something to say. Finally, having none of it and apparently perturbed with my point of view, he raised his hand and said forcefully, "So you're telling me that Bill Parcells, one of the greatest football coaches of all time, can't motivate his players?" Parcells, at the time, was head coach of the New England Patriots. Evidently I had drilled deep into this guy's nerve center – he was obviously a huge Parcells fan. "Yes," I said, "that's what I'm saying."

"That's ridiculous," he shot back. "Parcells wins everywhere he goes. He turns losing teams into winning teams. He makes great players out of average ones. How can you say he can't motivate his players to excel?"

"I agree with you," I countered. "Parcells does have a track record of success. That much is undeniable. But our point of departure is in how he does it. Parcells is successful leading others, not because he motivates them, but because he is able to inspire in them their individual sense of self-motivation. He isn't able to get the best out of them...he is able to get them to get the best out of themselves. It's their choice to respond, not Parcells's ability to force. The power of deciding to act, then actually taking action, rests with the players, not with Parcells. Further proof of this is that many leaders, Parcells included, have penalty systems when players don't comply with pre-stated rules – penalties like not starting a game, sitting out an entire game, suspensions for misbehavior, and monetary fines. Isn't it interesting that some players still violate the rules even while knowing in advance what the penalties are – while others do not. Why? Individual choice. Different levels of self-motivation. Parcels can't *make* anybody do anything. No leader can. Each individual decides for himself." Anyway, that's what I told him, but I still think the guy didn't like my answer because, in his mind, I was attacking one of his heroes.

Wright

Interesting viewpoint. So what's the next step? In other words, once a person accepts responsibility for self-motivation – not expecting it to come from outside – how does he or she parlay that into a successful outcome?

Houcek

By doing what all successful people do: *taking action*. That one secret is the springboard to more achievement than any other single
factor. And the lack of it – the unwillingness to move, to go, to do, to
get up off your duff and act – is the <u>real</u> cause of most of life's dissatisfaction, anger, and frustration that gets mistakenly attributed to
other causes.

And that drives me nuts. Listening to a whiner moan and com-
plain about how he doesn't get any breaks, everyone is against him,
and nothing goes his way, is pure self-pity, founded on nothing fac-
tual. Hey, winners suffer from all the same setbacks losers do – they
just handle it differently. Winners swing into high gear and take action; losers get that deer-in-the-headlights look and freeze. Then to
save face, they start that hideous blaming, finger-pointing, complain-
ing, griping, poor-me routine. Whiners, moaners, and complainers get
no one's respect.

But let's get back to the winners – because the model for success
rides with them. What two traits do winners have that leapfrog them
ahead of the pack? One, a bias for action. And two, a willingness to
fail. Can't really have one without the other.

Wright

Talk more about that. There are so many conflicting opinions on
failure – on whether it's a source of discouragement or whether it has
some positive value. What's your take on failure?

Houcek

I have two strong opinions on failure.

One is, to win, you have to be willing to let failure happen. Not
just to <u>risk</u> failure, but to *actually* fail...to be embarrassed, to look
foolish, to have your family, best friends, and business associates
think you're an idiot. It'll happen anyway, so you might as well accept
it, not fight it, and get comfortable with it. When you increase your
volume of action, you simultaneously increase your rate of failure –
it's inevitable. The more you do, the more you fail. Winners fail much
more frequently than losers do, a fact that surprises losers. So think
about this: winners don't win more frequently just because they're
good; but because they make more attempts.

I don't believe all the very best baseball players in the world are in
the major leagues. Many are, but many more are there because they
outlasted the better ones who quit too soon. They had greater staying

power, even if not better talent. Same is true for the NFL, NBA, NHL, and all professional sports. Same is also true in business and life. Persistence ultimately wins – but you have to be willing to fail a lot to get there. Robert Fulton overcame mounds of public ridicule when he proclaimed he would invent a steam-powered boat – criticism from people who believed it could never be done – but he pressed on anyway and succeeded. Sports team managers call controversial plays in crucial situations that bear strong risk of failure – and many plays do fail, in front of thousands of fans. Those managers knew the risk and did it anyway.

Second – and after all this failure talk, it'll surprise you – I don't even believe in failure. Doesn't exist. In my value system, there is no failure, only undesirable outcomes from which we learn, grow, and improve. We remember Thomas Edison for, among other things, inventing electric light. But he failed some 10,000 times before he finally succeeded. Think about it, his failure-to-success rate was 10,000 to 1 – and yet we remember him for *successfully* inventing electric light, not for his many more attempts that didn't work, which most people have never even heard about. In fact, he was quoted as saying, *"I successfully invented 10,000 ways electric light wouldn't work."* How's that for a positive attitude? We forgive failure if it leads to an eventual success. Heck, we practically ignore it. Boston Red Sox fans are in such a high state of elation over winning the 2004 World Series, they're willing to virtually forgive the frustrating eighty-six-year wait from the last one. So sticking with it, when others fold their tent, often produces an eventual victory, and gets you labeled "successful."

Another example: look at the best golfers throughout history – Jack Nicklaus, Arnold Palmer, Tiger Woods, Phil Mickelson, and a cadre of others. How many times have you watched any one of them on television shank shots in tournament play – often many times in a single round – only to slowly, methodically, one stroke at a time, weave their way back into contention, then into the lead, and eventually to victory? It happens all the time.

In life, very seldom does everything go your way. There are always obstacles and problems. Bottom line, if you want to win more, quit seeing all the undesirable outcomes along the way as deal-killing failures. Because you'll also start to see yourself as a failure. Don't go there. An undesirable outcome is nothing more than one new piece of valuable information on the road to an eventual success – *if you stay with it.*

So the lessons are: to win, you have to be willing to look like a jerk. And you have to disavow failure as a concept.

Wright

That "looking like a jerk" thing is very real. It's scary ground for many people. Isn't that what causes people to hold back...to *not* go for the gold...to *not* pursue their most ambitious life dreams?

Houcek

It's a huge part of it, yes. But strangely, fear of failure often "masks" the *real* culprit...fear of <u>success</u>. It may seem odd that anyone could be uneasy about success because we connect it with achievement, joy, pride, glory, and money – and who doesn't want those? But fear of success happens all the time. Here's why. There's an unconscious conversation inside our heads that goes like this: *"If I succeed at this, everyone will know I can do it and will never accept less from me again. Expectations of me will elevate. So I can't be my comfortable, safe, happy-go-lucky, fun-loving self again. I don't need that pressure – I think I'll just fail at this and keep everyone's expectation of me low. Then, when I occasionally succeed, everyone will think I'm a hero. That, I can live with."*

The three percent who are the constant winners have found a way to override that conversation in their heads, to not let it control them, to ignore or eliminate it from their thinking. But the masses who, as Thoreau said, "lead lives of quiet desperation," trudge on, unaware that conversation is happening, wondering why nothing ever seems to go their way.

And the worst part is, failure is often easy to live with – because it brings out sympathy, understanding and support from our family, co-workers and friends. "Oh, it's okay, you gave it your best shot. Don't feel bad," they'll say. Or, "Hey, it just wasn't in the cards for you. Who needs that much responsibility anyway?" Mostly, people who offer these supportive statements, while well intentioned, are often dealing with that same "fear of success" demon themselves, and it's holding <u>them</u> back too. So their <u>un</u>spoken selfish feeling about you is: *"I really don't want you to succeed, because you'll blow past me, leave me in the dust, and won't want to be my friend anymore. Stay back on my level with me."* That kind of friend, no one needs.

Wright

Okay, jump into what we can do about all this. For those serious about improving their lives and outcomes, serious about becoming more self-motivated, and serious about overcoming fear of both failure and success, what action steps can we take?

Houcek

Lots of things. First, recognize you probably have limiting beliefs. Get rid of them; they'll destroy any chance of success. Beliefs drive our decisions, and decisions drive our actions. So if you're not clear on what your deep-held beliefs are, look at your own actions – the things you <u>do</u> – they're your best clue to your beliefs. Here's an example: many people have limiting beliefs in the area of wealth. They think they are not deserving of money...that wealth is tied to greed...that rich people are all pompous jerks...or that since they were raised in a middle class family, they aren't entitled to grow beyond that without losing face in the family. So they self-sabotage, sometimes consciously, often <u>un</u>consciously. But they'd never admit it. Instead, they save face by ridiculing people who make lots of money, when secretly, they want to <u>be</u> those people so bad they can taste it. Why do they behave this way? Trace it all back to a limiting belief about money. Gotta get rid of limiting beliefs!

Another action is, learn to obey the impulse and act now. Losers can't pull the trigger. The more you build the habit of obeying impulses – even without all the information you think you need – the greater and faster your sense of self-motivation will develop. Nike's old ad slogan "Just do it" is a good mantra to follow. More often than not, we have the facts we need. And by taking action, whatever facts you don't have will reveal themselves as you go, so you can course-correct on the fly. The point is, don't over think. Do.

Another point. No plan ever survives its collision course with reality. As soon as you act, some things will not go as planned, forcing you to alter your next actions. This fear of derailment scares the living daylights out of many people – and keeps them couch-bound. Get over it. The best way to beat that fear is to face it head-on. The next time you feel it, take a deep breath, grit your teeth, and *move!* If you do this enough times, you'll see it's more painless than you ever thought – that failure isn't a given, that you can handle obstacles, that you can think on your feet. That's a tremendous spirit-lifter and eventually it'll drive you to greater self-confidence and inner motivation.

Here's one that's huge: get rid of negative people in your life. We all have a few surrounding us. The older I get, the more selective I become in whom I let into my inner circle of influence. I only invite caring, like-minded, success-driven winners who have my best interests at heart, because I have theirs at heart. Chronically negative people will drag us into their misery, if we let them. Don't. Remove them as influencers. And let me be clear: by "getting rid of them," I don't mean doing them harm, nor do I mean embarrassing or humiliating them. Always respect their human dignity. I simply mean, quit spending time with them, don't hang around them, give no credence to their advice, and ignore their negativity. If you have to spend time with them – like in a work environment where you don't control their employment – then you may have to tolerate their presence, but don't let them influence you. Sometimes you have to suck it up and sweat it out.

Wright

What about role models as a source of inspiration? Are they valuable in life development?

Houcek

They are when they're decent, ethical, high-achieving role models. Those who are boisterous, arrogant, and unethical, aren't. Role models are best when they are *mentors* who work directly with you, on a frequent basis, often one-on-one, devoting focused time to you. I'm not talking about role models you know from a distance – like a pro athlete you admire but have never met.

I think learning from a mentor – the good kind – is the quickest and most intense of all ways to learn – better than anything else. And it's more focused too, since it's generally one-on-one. Other forms of learning are good, but less efficient, like classroom, books, tapes, CDs, videos, seminars, lectures, speeches, and others. While each of those has strong merit for the go-getter, none provide the ongoing, one-on-one benefits of a knowledgeable mentor. Hey, I give speeches, seminars and workshops all the time – and I've written other books – but I'll be the first to tell you that unless you have an accountability agent to hold your feet to the fire, those tools alone may not be enough. You may struggle with taking action because you have only yourself to depend on for a push. I always encourage clients to create their own five to eight-person Eagle Team of caring, like-minded, success-driven people who have their best interests at heart – and who will meet monthly for laser-focused discussion to help each other achieve personal and professional success. We're all more self-motivated with someone else to hold us accountable. Whether your mentor is one person, or a small group of dedicated people, it's an awesome arrow to have in your quiver.

Wright

What about obstacles along the way – those nasty nuisances that block us from accomplishing our task or getting what we want? How do they affect someone's self-motivation?

Houcek

Losers, a lot. Winners, very little. To a loser, an obstacle is another reason to feel sorry for himself and quit. To a winner, it's a source of new information from which to learn, grow, improve, and press on.

Here's a great way to look at obstacles. Consider an eagle. The same thing that prevents an eagle from faster flight – wind resistance – is what allows it to fly in the first place. No wind resistance, no flight. Can't fly in a vacuum. The point is, wind resistance is an obstacle. Yet without that obstacle, nothing happens. That's a metaphor for everything in life. Obstacles don't block us – they provide us with the energy, the fuel, and the knowledge we need to have anything we want. The next time something horrible happens to you that you think is trying to tell you to give up and go home, try re-directing your thoughts to this: *That roadblock was given to me as a gift – a golden opportunity to learn, grow and improve – and ultimately succeed – if I just hang with it.*

In his book and tapes, *Tough Times Never Last, But Tough People Do*, Dr. Robert Schuller devotes lengthy discussion to the subject of problems in life. He cites his beloved Crystal Cathedral in California as a perfect example. In its finished form, it's a beautiful, awe-inspiring structure. But getting to that end-point was a virtual nightmare of problem after problem. From before the first dirt was moved, through construction, all the way to the final build-out, it was fraught with every imaginable problem. If it could go wrong, it did. Every inch of the way, Dr. Schuller's mettle was tested, and with each obstacle, he faced a choice: give up or go on. While most people would have quit – and he was presented with hundreds of opportunities to throw in the towel along the way – he did not. Every obstacle was there for a reason. His job, he thought, was to figure out what, learn from it, and press on. He did. And the finished structure is proof of his tenacity, his self-motivation to overcome every obstacle, no matter how tumultuous.

Wright

Let's get back to other specific tools our readers can use to drive their own self-motivation. Give us more examples, please.

Houcek

In one of my other books, *Conversations on Success (Volume 4)*, I talk at length about finding your passions and living them every day...those things you make time for when no time exists...things you'll relentlessly spend time, energy, and money on in the pursuit of excellence...things that give you an empty feeling of loss when you can't make time or be your best...things that make your face light up and electrify your personality when you talk about them. Passions are a huge source of self-motivation. So many people lead lives that are boring, meaningless, and void of excitement. It's their fault, by the way, not the rest of the world's, which is who they usually blame. Anyway, get crystal clear on your passions and commit to living them every single day. Devote large blocks of time to them. This means, by the way, getting rid of non-passions, which is one of the healthiest things you can do. It's a worthy trade-off. Life is too short to settle for less.

In another of my books, *Success Is A Decision Of The Mind*, I lay out an entire systematized approach for life planning – which, taken in total, is the best formula I know for producing self-motivation. All the tools are right there, discussed in great detail. Let me briefly hit the high notes now.

Here are six of the biggest, that I haven't already mentioned in this interview: (1) get clear on your Life Mission – it's the core purpose you have for being on this planet, (2) discover your Core Behavioral Values – they are the best decision-making criteria you'll ever have and ever need, (3) keep an ongoing Master Want List – of everything you've ever wanted to be, do and have, (4) maintain a running list of Fulfilling Life Events – all your proud moments, rewarding accomplishments and goals achieved, (5) actively engage in Goal Setting – one of the most powerful human self-motivators, and (6) use Positive Affirmations every day – self-talk to fuel the fire of self-esteem. Now, don't leave any of this to chance or memory – buy a three-ring binder and create your own personal goal book, giving each of these elements its own tabbed section. Divide your life into eight areas and give each of them its own tabbed section too. The eight are: Career, Financial, Health, Family, Self Improvement, Spiritual, Adventure, and Business. This binder creates a systematized approach and requires time and attention on a regular basis – daily, weekly and monthly. Winners use systems to organize and simplify; losers shun them as "too much work." So be a winner and get this goal planning system in gear.

Speaking of goal setting, here are a few tips to make goals self-motivational and lower the odds of throwing in the towel half way through. First, commit your goal to one sheet of paper. Writing down your goal and all the other components I'm about to tell you, make it a real commitment. My rule of thumb is, unless and until you write it down, you're not serious – you're just fooling around.

Second, always set a deadline for completion, with a specific month-day-year. Human beings respond to deadlines, and the absence of one gives us no urgency to start.

Third, list out all the benefits that will come to you by achieving the goal. This is critical, because it ties to your level of passion. If there aren't enough compelling benefits to you, you may get derailed.

Fourth, think of the resources you'll need for successful completion – like skills, knowledge, tools, money, or support from others.

Fifth, think of what obstacles might come your way, and have an alternate action for each. This is contingency planning, and it's very important.

Sixth, always write out a step-by-step action plan with due dates for each action.

And last, proudly sign it at the bottom of the page. Your signature is a catalyst for emotional commitment – and launches you into action.

I go into greater detail on this "systematized life planning" approach in both of those other books, which, by the way, can be purchased off my web site, www.SoarWithEagles.com.

Wright

Rick, this has been a great interview, and I think our readers have lots of ideas to think about – and tools to work with. Any final thoughts?

Houcek

Yes, let me leave you with one more important tool for self-motivation.

Feedback – it's huge. It's easy to lose motivation because you're not getting feedback on how you're doing. Parents, teachers, coaches, bosses, co-workers, even spouses and friends – can all contribute to your <u>de</u>-motivation – if you'll let them – by not providing valuable feedback. There's a simple solution: *ask*. Don't rely on them to tell you; go ask them. And don't take their first answer, which is often a blow-off, I-don't-want-to-hurt-your-feelings answer. Keep asking, multiple times, going deeper each time.

A good rule of thumb is: ask the same question three times, three different ways, and take the third answer. Here's an example. Q1: How am I doing for you? Q2: If there were three things you wish I'd do more of, what would they be? Q3: What are my co-workers specifically saying about how I'm doing? Notice Q3 is from a third-party perspective, which gives the person you're asking permission to tell the truth, because it's presumably coming from others. Yet what you'll get is <u>his</u> opinion. In this three-question set, ignore the first two answers and pay attention to only the third – *it's* the most truthful answer. Oh, and one last point on feedback – all feedback isn't positive. You have to be willing to hear the bad with the good.

Wright

Thank you, Rick. Lots of meat our readers can sink their teeth into. Today we've been talking to Rick Houcek – keynote speaker, workshop leader, strategic planning facilitator, CEO coach, and author.

Rick, thanks for your valuable thoughts on *The Power of Motivation*.

Houcek

Self motivation, David. It's the only kind you control, and the only kind that matters. And thank *you*. It's been my pleasure.

About The Author

Rick Houcek

Rick Houcek's singular company purpose is: To provide high-octane, world-class strategic planning systems for business and life, helping Top Gun leaders, teams and individuals to succeed "on purpose, most of the time," rather than "by accident, some of the time." He does this four primary ways: (1) facilitating his Power Planning™ strategic planning retreats for small and mid-size companies, (2) leading his Passion Planning™ workshops for ambitious individuals on personal life planning and goal setting, (3) delivering high-energy motivational keynotes, and (4) one-on-one success coaching. He has coached entrepreneurs, CEOs, presidents, and senior executives for over 10 years, and is former president of Ross Roy Advertising, an Atlanta ad agency and division of the $700 million Ross Roy Group. A University of Missouri graduate, he is a member of the National Speakers Association and has been recognized in Who's Who Among U.S. Executives and Who's Who in Georgia. Rick is married and passionately devoted to his soul mate, adores his awesome grown twins, and has four fanatical life passions: his family, his personal health and fitness, helping others prosper through his business and friendships, and playing competitive baseball on a traveling men's team.

Rick Houcek, President
Soar With Eagles, Inc.
5398 Hallford Drive
Atlanta, Georgia 30338
Phone: 770.391.9122
Fax: 770.393.0076
Email: Rick@SoarWithEagles.com
www.SoarWithEagles.com